M000302279

IMPRESS
AND
INFLUENCE

HIGHLIGHTS AND INSIGHTS FOR PRACTICING INTENTIONAL MENTORSHIP

BHARAT MOHAN, PHD

Copyright © 2021 by Bharat Mohan, PhD
All rights reserved. No portion of this book may be reproduced in any
form or by any means, including electronic storage and retrieval
systems, except by explicit prior written permission of the author.
Brief passages excerpted for review and critical purposes are excepted.

Cloth ISBN: 978-1-0879-7884-0

This book is typeset in EB Garamond
Designed by Hannah Gaskamp

CONTENTS

CONTENTS

INTRODUCTION

PREDICTION AND DECISION

*W*hile I've had a number of positive influences and role models throughout my life, many of my attitudes, approaches, and actions in life have been shaped by the lessons I've learned from my "Prediction and Decision Shelf"—a row on my bookshelf dedicated to the fields of forecasting and decision science. If you can look into the future with some degree of accuracy, you have the opportunity to make more informed choices regarding upcoming decisions. After all, we'll take a quick look at a weather widget from time to time before getting dressed and stepping outside, right? And I can't possibly be the only one who checks a traffic app before heading out for a drive. Even when it comes to a child's education, projections on the futures of different industries and trends in earning potentials across different vocations have led parents to now look for ways to expose their children to STEM fields at younger ages. Our lives are a series of decisions and choices, all of which we have the potential to improve upon if we can accurately forecast and predict the future in some capacity.

The books on my Prediction and Decision Shelf, all of which I strongly endorse to anyone who asks for book recommendations, have helped improve my approach to both personal and team-level decision-making and forecasting. However, I think there's an important piece of the discussion missing from my years of studying these fields and reading these books. Even within my Prediction and Decision Shelf, I have yet to find any research-based approaches to explain how people use personal relationships to improve their ability to make decisions about their futures. So,

I set out to fill this gap—the intersection between decision science, forecasting, and developing genuine personal relationships with others to improve our skills in both of these areas. Simply put, I wanted to investigate the process of *mentorship*.

WHO THIS BOOK IS FOR

Building a valuable mentorship relationship requires hard work over a long period of time. This book will explore the details of that commitment and provide a timeline for building the relationship, from the perspectives of both the mentee and the mentor. The insights presented in this book are the result of rigorous qualitative research conducted with a diverse set of participants. The research design of this project was informed by focusing on diversity in the following ways:

- Diversity amongst the participants (age, sex, race/ethnicity, occupation, job sector, etc.)

- Diversity in the type of mentorship interactions the participants have experienced (peer mentorship, experienced mentor with an inexperienced mentee, etc.)

- Diversity in the topics of mentorship in which both parties engaged (personal mentorship, professional mentorship, or a combination of both)

I am confident that at least some of the takeaways presented in this book will be useful to you, regardless of where you are in your life's journey or the type of mentorship that would be of most use to you. It is important to note that some of the anecdotes and quotes in this book are anonymized, and others are properly attributed to the interviewee. In the latter case, I provide some background on these individuals so you can have useful insight into where they've come from, the fields in which they work, and the types of mentorship they either receive or provide.

Ultimately, this book was written for readers who want to be more *intentional* with their approach to mentorship. It's my hope that you'll feel more prepared to strategically work toward building a better future for yourself and others by using some of the best practices I've outlined in this book. I've provided prescriptive recommendations for both mentees and mentors to be more effective in their respective roles as they pursue a fulfilling mentorship relationship. My approach to the research allows for the findings in this book to be applied in a variety of scenarios:

- **Professional Mentorship**—supervisors providing mentorship for their direct reports; colleagues reciprocating mentorship with each other (either within teams or cross-functionally); or a mentee seeking mentorship from either someone at work or outside their organization

- **Personal Mentorship**—individuals giving and receiving mentorship to develop stronger relationships with family and friends; engaging in discussions about life decisions (including career) that align with the personal core values of the mentee; or faith-based/spiritual mentorship

- **Organizational Mentorship**—organizations looking to start a formalized mentorship program or improve the processes of an existing mentorship program

HOW THIS BOOK IS ORGANIZED

This book is divided into four parts. Certain parts may be more useful to you than others depending on the role you have (or intend to have) in a mentorship relationship, but I strongly recommend reading all sections of this book. Building genuine relationships with a mentor or mentee requires a holistic understanding of the roles and responsibilities of both parties. This book will provide you with nuances and dynamics that are important to consider as you engage in an efficient and effective mentor-mentee relationship. The following is a brief overview of the sections contained within this book.

PART I: IMPORTANT CONSIDERATIONS FOR MENTORSHIP

The opening section explains the considerations everyone should keep in mind when entering into a mentor-mentee relationship, regardless of the role they are in. The findings outlined in this section provide a lens through which individuals and organizations can view mentorship. This foundation helps set the stage for the insights and recommendations that will be made throughout the book.

PART II: HOW TO BE AN INTENTIONAL MENTEE

This section focuses specifically on the role of the mentee. There will be detailed recommendations on how mentees can improve their approach and put their best foot forward to impress potential mentors. The first three chapters will delve into the distinct phases that successful mentees will advance through to facilitate a valuable mentorship dynamic: *Preparation, Potential, and Progress.* The idea of *Preparation* includes information on what mentees need to know about themselves and how to strategically identify the right mentor for their goals and aspirations. *Potential* is the step in which mentees demonstrate to their mentors that they are not only prepared for the relationship but also have the potential for exponential growth when applying the lessons they learn from the mentor. *Progress* explores specific, long-term ways in which mentees can continue to drive the relationship forward. These three chapters will provide distinct recommendations for mentees who are looking for professional mentorship versus those who are looking for personal guidance.

The *Preparation, Potential, and Progress* chapters are process-oriented, in that they provide specific actions for mentees to take to influence the process of mentorship toward a more fulfilling outcome.

The final chapter of this section will outline the *Qualities of Good Mentees*. It will specify the mindsets, characteristics, and behaviors that successful mentors look for in an ideal mentee. This chapter is split into two sections: what mentors *initially* look for in mentees, and what mentors want to see mentees demonstrate *as the relationship progresses.*

PART III: HOW TO BE AN INTENTIONAL MENTOR

This section of the book will provide findings from the research that will help mentors be more intentional in their approach to the role. The first three chapters of this section will provide details on how successful mentors can provide mentees with value through *Patient Persistence, Perspective, and Problem Solving.* The concept of *Patient Persistence* says that mentors should focus on being both compassionate and consistent when they engage in a mentorship role. *Perspective* refutes the notion that the role of a mentor is to provide solutions to mentees; rather, it explains that the role of a mentor is to provide options and different paths for mentees to choose from. *Problem Solving* takes the previous two chapters a step further by providing a framework for mentors to help mentees build their own system of thinking for how they might creatively address challenges and obstacles.

The final chapter in this section will look at the *Qualities of Good Mentors.* In this chapter, I have outlined the characteristics and traits of good mentors, as identified in the responses of the mentees and mentors I interviewed. If you are reading this book to improve your approach to serving as a mentor, this chapter will be of particular interest, as it highlights feedback from mentees and reflections from the experiences of good mentors.

PART IV: OTHER SPECIAL CONSIDERATIONS

While I am confident in the value of the findings you will read about, I will never pretend that this book precludes any future work on the topic of mentorship—no research project can ever *fully* explain the phenomenon it set out to investigate. In fact, it is an expectation for research papers published in prestigious, peer-reviewed academic journals to include a section that acknowledges the limitations of the research. A number of research papers also acknowledge delimitations, which define the boundaries and limits of the research as a way to establish the scope of the project. Mentorship is an enormous topic to research correctly, and I felt it necessary to outline the delimitations of the research in Part IV. Several ancillary topics related to mentorship arose in the interviews I conducted, but I made the decision to focus on the subjects covered in the first three parts of the book.

I wanted to offer an overview of these delimitations for two reasons. First, I think it is important to provide a full picture of the details related to mentorship that surfaced in the interviews. Second, as I mentioned earlier, building valuable and authentic mentor-mentee relationships requires a commitment to hard work. This same philosophy should hold true for any research related to investigating a successful mentorship in action. An outline and brief discussion of these special considerations can serve as a jumping-off point for future research on topics related to mentorship.

PART 1

IMPORTANT CONSIDERATIONS FOR MENTORSHIP

CHAPTER 1

SETTING THE STAGE

The most fulfilling examples of mentorship are the ones in which both mentors and mentees play an active role in building the relationship. Mentors have the ability to use experiences from their past to improve the future of their mentees. Mentors can help map out the steps their mentees need to take to achieve their goals and accelerate toward a better future. Mentors also help mentees refine (and redefine) their goals on the basis of considerations the mentees were not previously thinking through. The support that mentors provide throughout the relationship is critical, as navigating the future requires embracing uncertainty; the ability to accept ambiguity is particularly difficult for some mentees, who equate guidance to being given structured formulas and concrete solutions to what they are asking for. Examples of big-picture decisions that mentors can help with include:

- Education choices (which college to attend, which classes to take, which major to declare, etc.)

- Career choices (where to work, which projects to take on, how to grow in their current role, how to position themselves for a promotion, etc.)

- Personal life decisions (whether or not to get married, renting versus buying a home, how to approach conversations with family members, how to improve personal relationships, etc.)

This is not an exhaustive list of ways in which a mentor can provide value to a mentee, but all of these scenarios require mentors to have keen insight and top-notch communication skills. The process of mentorship is even more nuanced when you consider that, in addition to helping mentees make decisions about the future, a strong mentor needs to be able to validate who the mentee currently is and where they are in their lives. Striking this balance is not a task for the uncommitted or the dispassionate.

While mentors are responsible for driving many aspects of the mentorship process, there are ways in which mentees can take the lead. As the party that is receiving guidance, it is important for mentees to be aware that the most effective relationships are ones in which the mentee practices leadership at various points of the relationship-building process. Just as our deepest friendships and familial bonds require both people to play active roles in facilitating the relationship, so too should *both* mentors and mentees proactively contribute to building a meaningful connection.

The idea for this book came from a conversation I had while attending the Northwest Basketball Coaches Forum. After a summer of high-profile college basketball coaches speaking on the technical aspects of offensive strategy, defensive principles, and team management techniques, one attending coach voiced an interest in learning more about how to pursue mentorship (namely how to network with and receive guidance from these well-known coaches). Approaching the mentee role with intention and strategy is an important part of developing valuable mentorship relationships.

As I outlined in the Introduction, this book comprises distinct sections of recommendations specific to mentees and the best practices unique to mentors. However, it's important to set the stage in Part I for considerations that both mentees and mentors should keep on their radars and be mutually responsible for as they develop a relationship. This chapter outlines five major findings of the research—in order of importance—that everyone engaging in the mentorship process should consider.

HAVE TO VERSUS GET TO

I'll give two spoilers on what will be discussed more in-depth in Parts II and III of this book, respectively. Spoiler alert No. 1: One of the qualities an ideal mentee should possess, as identified by successful mentors, is a growth and learning mindset. Spoiler alert No. 2: One of the qualifications of a good mentor is having relevant subject matter expertise and experience. You probably nodded along as you read the two spoilers, as these findings are intuitive and straightforward. However, neither of these findings matter without both the mentor and mentee demonstrating the most essential quality needed for mentorship: being a "get to" rather than a "have to."

Most people who come through our lives (either for a reason, a season, or a lifetime) broadly belong to one of these two categories. We all have people in our lives for whom we think, *I have to respond to this* when you see an incoming text or call from them. These relationships are distinctly different from the ones where you feel like you *get to* spend time with the person—you *get to* learn about them, ask them questions, hear their answers, share laughs, and create memories. Both mentees and mentors fundamentally want the other person to be someone with whom they are excited to go through the process of building a relationship.

During the five months I conducted research interviews for this book, I couldn't help but notice the smiles that crept across the faces of the interviewees as they recalled specific experiences, conversations, and connections they shared with their mentor or mentee. While many relationships are transactional, the mentors and mentees I spoke to viewed the relationships as *transformational*. There was no question as to the level of appreciation they had for the other person. The prevailing sentiment was that the mentorship relationship they were reflecting on did not feel like a chore. There was genuine, palpable gratitude for the opportunity to build something special with the other person.

So, how do you put your best foot forward and become a "get to"? You might be thinking, *It just happens organically. There are some people I click with, and it just works out.* You're absolutely right: there are certain aspects of fulfilling relationships that we can't control, yet they seem natural and just *feel* right. But that doesn't mean we can't be as intentional as possible in the relationship-building process. As one of the interview participants so eloquently said, "The details of each relationship may vary, but the underlying goal of each meeting between a mentor and mentee should be for both people to be excited for the next meeting. I think if both people thought about ways to make the other person excited about the next meeting, they'd find some simple ways to build a deeper relationship."

"Get to" people are the ones who do the right things, even when they don't have to. One of the mentees I interviewed reflected on the time when she was a young social worker in a hospital and her mentor (the Medical Director of hospice care) went above and beyond to ensure that she had a "seat at the table" in decision-making. The fact that her mentor practiced such behaviors, when the culture of the healthcare field is often one in which doctors do not prioritize the inclusion of younger females whose expertise is in social work, helped her develop a strong connection to her mentor.

A different mentee, who is currently a sports agent, relayed a memory of why he values his mentor so much. "I've known my mentor since I was a kid and he was in his early twenties. I'm almost forty now, so we've known each other for a while. My mentor is currently a highly successful financial advisor," he said. "What I really appreciate about him is that, from time to time, he'll give me a call and tell me about a challenging situation that came up in his work and he had to deal with. While the details of our work are different, he connects the dots; he can see that what he's going through might apply to me in my work at some point. Even while he's going through his own stuff, he has the presence of mind to call me and tell me about it, just to keep it on my radar in case it's something that'll help me in my future.

"Who knows if it'll ever come up for me. Who knows if it's something I'll be dealing with a year from now, ten years from now, or twenty years from now. If it does, though, I'll be ready. I have some notes about the call I had with him and how he dealt with [challenges] sitting in my drawer. Calling me just in case it's something that's helpful in my future—that's just him doing the right thing, even when he doesn't have to. Things like that really make me look forward to staying in touch with him and keeping the relationship going."

In interviews with mentors, I heard stories about saving thoughtful, handwritten cards their mentees had sent them over the years. While these mentees didn't have to take the time to handwrite a card expressing gratitude for the value the mentor has provided them over the years, it is appreciated. This small example of mentees doing the right thing even when they don't have to helps mentors continue to be excited about investing in the relationship.

The insights in Part II (for mentees) and Part III (for mentors) will help you build toward being viewed as a "get to" type of person. Simply starting with the goal of being viewed by others as a "get to" person (as opposed to only demonstrating a learning/growth mindset as a mentee or merely relying on your subject matter expertise as a mentor) is a powerful shift in the right direction as you move toward building a successful mentorship dynamic.

CONSISTENCY

Both mentors and mentees I interviewed cited the importance of *consistency* from the other person in the relationship. As a mentor or a mentee, you might be striving for perfection in your role. However, consistency is far more valuable than perfection. In some relationships, mentors add the most value just by being consistently available and present. One mentor I interviewed went to the hospital when the father of his mentee passed away from cancer. Even as a spiritual guide, confidant, and trusted advisor for his mentee, he didn't have a clue as to what to say in that situation. As he reflected on it, he told me he realized that he didn't need to have any words. By just showing up and being present during an emotional and vulnerable time for his mentee, the mentor provided the most amount of value possible. Make no mistake that it wasn't just being there at the hospital this one time; having *consistently* been available to his mentee over many years, the mentor made himself the right person to provide support in this time of need.

My research elicited many similar stories within different contexts, including: an adult working in the security department at the local public schools whose presence literally saved the lives of several young people by steering them away from risky situations; youth basketball coaches at a local community center, whose regular availability kept young mentees away from gang involvement and violence; lawyers who enacted an "open door at all times" policy for newly minted law school graduates to utilize for guidance and advice as they transitioned to practicing law; and a doctor who routinely offered invitations to the staff social worker to connect about hospice care ideas. These are just a few of the examples I heard about. Regardless of the circumstances and the varying levels of active involvement that mentors took in these situations, the common theme was the importance of consistency.

Regularity in availability, being present, and invitations to connect are not the only types of consistency required of a good mentor. Those providing mentorship also need to be consistent in how they treat all people, regardless of context, power dynamic, position, title, or type of relationship. Mentors must demonstrate consistent behaviors in all situations to build the trust of mentees. In the interviews I conducted, mentees across the board agreed that there is no shortage of experts in their respective fields. But what sets a good mentor apart are integrity and character—two traits that require consistency over time.

On the flip side, mentees must also demonstrate consistency in their commitment to not only the relationship with their mentors but also their desire to grow as a result of the mentorship they receive. The best mentees are the ones who regularly reach out to their mentors and continue to push the relationship forward. Even as they do this, mentors want to see consistency in their mentees' drive and ambition to achieve their goals. Essentially, an ideal mentee moves from being *motivated* to being *disciplined*.

Motivation is dynamic; it goes up and down depending on the level of commitment to the original goal. If the outcome is "out of sight, out of mind," then motivation fades. A disciplined mentee, however, always practices the right behaviors, regardless of how close or far they are from their goals—because it's the right thing to do.

I can't stress this enough: Mentorship requires commitment to hard work over a long period of time. Mentees must demonstrate that they are willing to consistently work hard so that their mentors will continue pouring into the relationship. In addition to demonstrating consistency, mentees must show over time that they are applying what they have learned from their mentor. Consistency in behavior by both mentors and mentees is critical to building trust in the relationship.

OBSERVE AND EXPERIENCE

When I first started this project, I assumed that the most useful findings would inform specific, detailed recommendations to help facilitate conversations between mentors and mentees. What I found, however, was that conversations were of secondary importance. The primary way in which mentors and mentees create a fulfilling relationship is by having the opportunity to *observe and experience* how the other person approaches problem solving and their critical thinking process. A number of the interviewees— both mentors and mentees—talked about the art of "always having your antennae up."

Mentors must pay close attention to not just the words of their mentee but their actions. Good mentors are the ones who triangulate information on the basis of what their mentee tells them directly, insights they receive about their mentee from sources within their network, and making sense of the behaviors their mentee exhibits when observing them. It's important for mentors to keep in mind that most mentees *don't know what they don't know*; mentees don't have complete clarity on what to ask for or ways in which a mentor can help them. By observing their mentee in action, a mentor can leverage their own expertise to help fill in these gaps and provide more value to their mentee.

One mentor I talked to provides personal life mentorship. Because this mentor-mentee pair views each other as a "get to" and have been close friends for more than twenty-five years, the mentor is able to openly provide feedback about the mentee's parenting skills. By observing the parenting approach of his mentee, the mentor was able to point out blind spots in his own parenting style that led to treating his children differently. This difference in treatment were ways in which his children could have perceived as unfair. The mentor communicated this feedback to his mentee in a tactful, respectful, and nonjudgmental manner in order for his mentee to receive it in a productive way. Without the ability to observe his mentee in action, the mentor would not have been able to provide the same value through discussion and conversation.

Mentees who are intentional in being present and fully engaged when interacting with their mentor can benefit by observing their mentor in action, making sense of these observations, and then using these interpretations in conversations. Mentors are impressed by mentees who indicate they have been paying attention outside of discussions and direct interactions. Mentees can send these signals by citing specific language used, actions taken, or general patterns they have noticed about the mentor that they respect, like, or are curious about. This helps the conversation reach greater depths than if the mentee did not observe the mentor at all. For example, one of the mentees I interviewed spoke about his first basketball coaching job in his early twenties. He worked for a highly respected AAU program and observed his mentor (a more experienced coach and the AAU Program Director) at practices. The mentee made it a point to not waste opportunities for interaction by asking only surface-level questions. Instead, he committed to making sure that the times he spoke to his mentor, especially early on, were chances to learn something deeper and more insightful.

This mentee was able to answer the surface-level questions for himself simply by paying attention to the drills his mentor ran in practice, the expectations he set for players in the program, and how he conducted himself. This freed up the mentee to spend time asking his mentor more program-level questions, such as how to secure sponsorship deals with companies. The mentee took what he learned from his mentor and applied it to an AAU program he started eight years later. He was able to not only run the program the right way (with appropriate core values and expectations of players) but also secure a sponsorship deal with Under Armour. The level of success the mentee achieved with the AAU program he started (which featured multiple future Division I players and a recent NBA first-round draft pick) can be traced back to the hours spent intentionally observing his mentor in action. This observation opened the door to hold deeper conversations in a faster timeframe.

In another example, a former Admiral in the United States Navy told me that, early in his career, he saw that his mentor was taking the initiative to start an internal written communication about the job analyses he conducted. Observing and experiencing his mentor in action by reading these publications provided him with advantages as a mentee. He was able to demonstrate to his mentor that he had read his communication in great depth, vocalize appreciation for the hard work the mentor put in, and ask very specific questions about the analyses the mentor had conducted. These steps helped garner the trust of his mentor and build their relationship. Additionally, the former Admiral was able to find meaning in the way his mentor processed the information that appeared in the final version of the internal publication.

This reflective exercise helped him clarify the ways in which he had a similar thought process to his mentor, as well as the ways in which he was different. As the relationship progressed, he was able to discern between the advice from his mentor that he would adopt and adapt versus the feedback that would not work for him. What's clear is that it is always a best practice, both as a mentor and a mentee, to commit to observing and experiencing the way the other party operates when the opportunities present themselves.

THE BALANCE BETWEEN FORMAL AND INFORMAL

This finding is, in some ways, a blend of being a "get to" type of person and practicing *consistency*, regardless of whether you are a mentor or a mentee. It is the responsibility of both parties to make the other person feel as if the relationship is mutually beneficial and fulfilling. This is a harder goal to achieve than you might think, owing to the tradeoffs of *formality and informality* in the relationship. Having a purely formal connection adds credence to the belief that the mentor is engaging in the relationship to "check the box" or for self-indulgent reasons. Adding a level of formalization to the relationship also makes it harder to judge whether the mentee is intrinsically motivated to succeed, or whether they are only doing the right things because the high degree of structure provided for them in a formalized relationship makes it easy for them to practice the right behaviors. Remember, mentors want mentees who are disciplined and likely to be successful regardless of context or environment. It's not *true* mentorship if the mentee is only succeeding under a narrow set of constraints.

However, a purely informal type of mentorship risks losing the frequency of meetings and interactions needed to capitalize on the momentum necessary to drive the relationship forward. It's easy to have a great meeting with someone, leave it open ended for when the next meeting will be, and then several months pass until you connect again. Riding the wave of the momentum created by a great conversation or interaction, particularly early in the relationship, is critical in creating a sustainable mentor-mentee bond.

So, how should you go about balancing the formal and informal? A Technology Consultant told me that he and his mentor would set aside time every week to talk over lunch about his career trajectory, but it would never be at the same day or time each week. Rather than formally scheduling a weekly hour-long meeting on their calendars and coming prepared with an agenda, they mutually committed to making time for each other every week in an informal way. Another pair of interviewees who at the time worked as administrators at an Ivy League university, told me that they met at the same café on campus as part of their mentor-mentee relationship. The mentee described a process by which she reached out to her mentor every few weeks to discuss work-related topics. While the day and time never followed any pattern, they carved out the same physical space on campus that served as a safe, familiar, and comfortable environment for their conversations.

The same balance applies if you engage in mentorship with kids and young adults. A handful of participants in the research study for this book volunteered their time every Sunday night for more than five years (talk about consistency!) to provide kids in their community with a safe, productive alternative to how they may otherwise choose to spend their time. The location, day, and time were the same every week over the course of five years, but the activities provided for the kids varied from week to week.

The hard work, time commitment, and strategy required to balance the formal with the informal in all these examples demonstrate that, when both parties take intentional steps to strike this equilibrium, trust is built between the mentor and mentee—whether it's two adults engaging in professional mentorship or a group of adults showing hundreds of young kids that they are worth such a high level of consideration and attention.

PHYSICAL SPACE CONSIDERATIONS

The upcoming chapters will provide adaptive approaches to how mentors and mentees can take steps to create space for trust, vulnerability, openness, and other abstract constructs that are integral to high-functioning mentorship. An interesting finding on physical space considerations for conversations between mentors and mentees provides a technical piece to contemplate.

In the interviews I conducted, there were clear connections between the physical space in which mentors and mentees conducted their conversations and the topics they discussed. Awareness of this connection can allow you, whether you are a mentor or a mentee, to be more intentional with how you approach discussions with the other party. The overall finding is that the physical space where the conversation takes place primes the topics being discussed.

In the case of professional mentorship, conversations in a conference room or within the office tend to revolve around technical aspects of the projects the mentee is working on. When mentors and mentees leave the office, whether it is to grab lunch or walk to a coffee shop, they focus more on the big picture: the career trajectory/career goals of the mentee (promotions, internal transfer to a different team, external opportunities, etc.).

Personal-life mentorship was also explored in this research project. One mentor I interviewed told me that she views invitations to sit at her dining table for dinner as a way to build a sense of community. Her mentee told me in a separate interview that being at the dinner table in the home of her mentor helped facilitate and drive their relationship forward. Being in the physical space of someone else's home, particularly a potential personal-life mentor, allows the mentee to observe and experience how the mentor operates at home. This opportunity helps the mentee build trust in the mentor and gives them the confidence to ask for advice on topics such as relationships, navigating college (both within and outside of the classroom), and even have deeper discussions about spirituality and other big-picture subjects.

This insight is something to keep in mind as you approach mentorship. For example, if you are the coach of a sports team and you are looking to mentor your team captain, be intentional about having conversations related to leadership and building team chemistry at the field or court where your team plays. However, if the topic of conversation is the importance of academics and being eligible to stay on the team, be intentional about holding that conversation in a classroom setting or an academic advising office.

Alternatively, if you are the one seeking professional guidance, make sure you take physical space considerations into account on the basis of the type of conversation you want to have. As a lawyer, you'd want to stay at the office or the courthouse to discuss specific strategies of how to approach a case. However, you might suggest grabbing a drink after work or going for a walk with a fellow attorney who has vocalized feeling burned out and talk through tips of how to practice self-care in a high-pressure job. If a more experienced coworker is nice enough to meet with you at your request and sends a calendar invite for a meeting in a conference room, don't be afraid to suggest lunch at a restaurant or a walk to the nearest coffee shop (while offering to pay!) if you want to discuss your career in broader terms. This is an appropriate setting to discuss topics like how best to position yourself for a promotion, as opposed to specific technical details of projects you are working on.

I would be remiss if I didn't provide suggestions on how to adapt physical space considerations to an increasingly virtual world, given that some of the practices we are currently engaging in are likely permanent. (As I write this, I haven't had an in-person meeting with my business partner or a client in more than a year!) I have recommended to several of my clients that they consider priming virtual calls with their coworkers, direct reports, and teams by being thoughtful of the background image they use for the call. For example, I have suggested that they make their background the logo of their organization, a picture of their office building, or one that contains the mission and vision statements of their company. This is a small step that takes minimal effort but could produce positive results in facilitating a team meeting.

One person I interviewed specializes in mindset training for teenagers. When speaking to kids at different schools or to members of a community organization such as the YMCA, he has made it a point to switch his Zoom background to the physical building of the school the kids attend or to the specific YMCA where the kids are members. I have also heard stories of people who have participated in Zoom Happy Hours with friends from college. It's common for the friends on the call to set their background as their favorite college dive bar or the off-campus house where they all lived together, as if to connect the places where they first had drinks together to the drinks they were currently enjoying, albeit virtually.

Although this is based solely on anecdotal feedback with no hard data in terms of the effectiveness of these actions, my clients and my friends have continued to be intentional about the virtual background they set depending on the audience and the topic of conversation. Some of you may not be sold on the value of physical space considerations or on being intentional with virtual backgrounds. You might be thinking, *You said from the outset that engaging in mentorship requires commitment to hard work over a long period of time. This seems like a small detail to care about compared to all the other considerations.* Honestly, in many ways, you would be right. But I think it's important to include this insight from the research for one specific reason: taking this consideration into account requires literally no risk and no cost. The time you have to spend to be intentional about this is minimal. You might as well keep it in mind and consider the best type of meeting location, just to see if it helps in facilitating the conversation.

These five findings are a mix of adaptive and technical considerations for mentorship that set the stage for the remaining sections of the book. Their importance can't be overstated. As you make meaning of your own experiences and approaches to mentorship, be sure to pay close attention to these five insights. They're important because they are not dependent on the type of mentorship in which you engage or the role you play in the relationship.

PART II

HOW TO BE AN INTENTIONAL MENTEE

CHAPTER 2

PREPARATION

The first stage of intentionally approaching your role as a mentee involves spending the necessary time and effort in *preparation* for the relationship with your mentor. The Preparation stage of your journey encompasses all the behind-the-scenes work that goes into setting yourself up for the best chance at a fulfilling relationship with your mentor.

KNOW YOURSELF

In the song "Wait for It" from the *Hamilton* musical, the character of Aaron Burr sings the line, "I am the one thing in life I can control." It certainly isn't easy, but the first step in preparing to be a mentee is just that—focusing on the one thing you can control: *knowing yourself.* As a mentee, you do *not* necessarily have all the fully formed and finalized ideas about yourself, and one of the responsibilities of a mentor is to help you understand yourself better. However, in order to be an intentional mentee, you *do* want to give some level of thought as to how you define yourself before connecting with your mentor. As you prepare for your role, spend some time practicing reflection and introspection in the following areas of self-awareness:

Core values: The best place to start is to have a good sense of your personal values. A strong understanding of your core values will give you clarity as to which recommendations from your mentor you're willing to adopt and which pieces of advice won't work for you. My business partner and I work a lot with our clients in helping them clearly identify their core values (three to five beliefs that are crucial to who you are and how you define yourself, and which will never change) versus their flex values (beliefs that you are willing to compromise on, depending on the context and situation). Even those who have achieved high levels of success can have difficulty articulating their values in a clear and succinct manner. They often have a general, abstract sense of their values but have not found the right language to express these thoughts. While you don't need absolute clarity on your core values before meeting with a potential mentor, it is in your best interest to prepare with the clearest language possible about what you believe your core values to be. Having as clear an idea as possible about the core values that guide your actions—as well as thoughts on how you define those values—is a great jumping-off point for discussions with a potential mentor. You can also use this knowledge to assess if there is alignment between your core values and those of your mentor.

Strengths and weaknesses: It's extremely important for you as a mentee to be able to not only identify your areas of strength but also areas where you have opportunity for improvement. You need to strike a balance between confidence in your ability to succeed and a level of humility needed for improvement. One role that mentors play is to be the one to "hold up a mirror" to mentees with honest feedback. This honesty serves the dual purpose of refuting your unfounded insecurities and getting you to accept that there are areas in your personal development that would benefit from a little bit of work. If you're prepared with an honest, realistic, and accurate assessment of your strengths and weaknesses, you'll not only make your mentor's job easier but you'll receive a deeper level of value from the mentorship relationship more quickly.

The youngest person I interviewed for this book (fifteen years old at the time) is an example of someone who has a good understanding of his strengths and weaknesses. He told me that he has always led by example amongst his peers, but there was an opportunity for improvement in his ability to serve as a vocal leader when needed. This young man's understanding of a strength and an opportunity for improvement was not unlike the awareness possessed by adults I interviewed, which included consultants, higher education administrators, and K-12 educators. All of these interview participants recognize the link between honest self-assessment of strengths and weaknesses and the next phase of knowing yourself: being clear about your goals.

Clarity of goals: Part of your behind-the-scenes work in preparing for mentorship is knowing what you would like to achieve. Concrete goals provide a level of context for your potential mentor about what they can focus on and how best to support you as you move toward your goals. Understanding your goals also helps you identify the type of person who would be the most effective mentor for you (the important components of what to look for in a mentor will be explained later in this chapter). A question to consider when thinking about your goals is, "What do I want the takeaways to be after meeting with my mentor?"

I interviewed an MBA student who spends time mentoring undergraduate students. "I generally make sure I have a lot of patience with the students I mentor," she told me. "Some of them are first-generation students, and sometimes mentees just don't know what they don't know. Working with young people who are just starting their college experience, I make sure that I remember what it was like to be in their shoes and to be learning some of the skills that are second nature to me now. That being said, I appreciate it when the students come prepared for our meetings. Part of that preparation is knowing what they want.

"I have a really fulfilling mentorship relationship with a student right now who's interested in finance. That isn't my background or my future career, but I know people who I can connect him with. Finance is obviously a general area, but he had specific areas within the industry that he was interested in moving toward. His clarity around that goal helped me introduce him to a couple of people I know who would be useful for him to talk to and learn more about the industry and hopefully land an internship. By having a pretty clear idea of his own goals, he helped me be as useful as I could be to him."

It should be noted that clarity of goals is not the same as *having* specific goals. This point is most clearly illustrated by an anecdote that came from an interview I conducted with a Product Manager at Google who previously worked as a User Experience Designer. In her spare time, she volunteers for a nonprofit that is committed to increasing the representation of women in STEM by providing mentorship for females who are either pursuing careers in the technology sector or who are navigating next steps in their current tech careers.

"Goals are a funny thing," she explained. "You need to know what you want out of your career and what your goals are before you talk to your mentor, but there's a balance you need to have. On the one hand, if you tell me you want to work at Google but have no idea whether you'd rather be a User Experience Designer or a Product Manager, I don't really know what I can do to help. Simply wanting to work at Google isn't enough for me to be able to provide you with value.

"On the other hand, it's counterproductive to have super-narrow goals. If one of the mentees at the nonprofit where I volunteer told me that they want to be a VP of Product Management at a company with more than a thousand employees within the next ten years . . . I mean, it's a great goal to have, but I think it limits how much value and perspective I might be able to provide. Part of being a good mentee is remaining open-minded and following your passions. That kind of specific goal limits your open-mindedness in a lot of ways. I think mentees should have some general parameters that broadly outline what they would like to achieve and ideas of where they would like to go, but they should make sure they aren't overly detailed in their goals."

A common theme I found in my interviews was that mentors want mentees who have goals that relate to *helping others*. From a professional standpoint, this might be "I want to be as successful in my job as I can be, not just to put myself in the best position for a promotion, but so that I can provide the highest level of service for my clients." In terms of a personal-life mentorship, a good mentor might appreciate the goal of "I want to be as good a parent as possible for my kids." Connecting the dots on how your goals are for more than just your own personal benefit is an important action to take as a mentee.

Today before tomorrow: People place an emphasis on the future when thinking about mentorship. While that thinking makes sense, it's important to not forget about your responsibilities to present obligations. Part of setting the stage for a successful mentorship relationship is making sure you're taking the necessary steps to be successful in your current situation. You can't focus on tomorrow if you don't have today figured out. Mentors won't be willing to bet on you and your future if you aren't presently engaging in the right behaviors. As one mentor I interviewed put it, "I can't mentor you and help you get into medical school if you're only doing the work to get a 1.6 GPA!"

I interviewed a mentee who attended the University of Pennsylvania for his undergraduate degree. He graciously allowed me to interview him as part of my research for this book, and he told me he had the perfect person to connect me with—his mentor during college. Being aware of this interviewee's chosen career after graduation, I figured his mentor would be a lawyer, political figure, or professor. Instead, the mentee connected me to Dan Harrell, who was the custodian of the Palestra (the historic home gym of the UPenn basketball teams) from 1989 to 2012.

The story of "Palestra Dan" is one of legend (he claims to have kicked NBA legend Julius Erving off the floor for wearing loafers instead of basketball shoes while shooting around). In addition to spending twenty-three years waking up at 4:00 AM to mop the floor of the Palestra in his iconic blue shorts, white socks, and gold spray-painted shoes, Dan spent a decade taking night classes at the university and graduated from UPenn with a degree in 2000. At his commencement ceremony, he walked across the graduation stage with a mop in hand to show the "housekeepers, mechanics, and electricians that it was one of us going down [to walk across the stage]." Understandably, Dan has been invited to speak at a number of university events to provide perspective and insight for current students. The university even had custom Dan Harrell bobblehead dolls made, one of which his mentee proudly showed me during our interview.

"Getting accepted into the University of Pennsylvania, it's all about how you can separate yourself and how you can be unique," Dan's mentee explained to me. "But then you get to college, you look around, and everyone is just like you. Everyone else in your class had a perfect score on their SAT, a 4.6 GPA in high school, and they're all striving for the same things: the next internship, the next job, the next promotion. What makes Dan special is that he did his job like it's the most important job on the planet, every single day. He mopped the floor at the Palestra the same way every time—it was always perfection. What I learned from him is that whatever job you have, be the best on the planet at it. Don't focus so much on the next job or the next goal; just be in the moment.

"Some people think Dan spent his time in night classes to get a degree and then go get another job. That was never his outlook. He took his night classes because he figured that he'd make the most out of his time on campus. It was never about the next goal for him. He was always telling me to focus on the job in front of me and make the most out of what I was doing, and that everything would take care of itself. He literally lived that outlook every single day. Out of anyone I met in college, Dan gave me the most unique perspective. No job is too big or too small to do to perfection, and that's something I've carried with me."

STRATEGICALLY IDENTIFYING A MENTOR

After you have worked to have a better understanding of yourself and the ways in which you operate, the next step in preparing for a mentorship relationship is to strategically identify potential mentors. Many people feel pulled to develop relationships with and receive mentorship from individuals who are well-known or have the most impressive titles. While I understand the logic behind wanting to learn from "the best," the findings from my research are clear: "the best" tends to come from mentors who are easily *accessible*, readily *available*, and effortlessly *approachable*. Rather than chasing the biggest names at UPenn (a school where it's not hard to find big names), Dan Harrell's mentee focused on finding a mentor who was always there to provide the perspective he needed as he navigated college. If you accept that the three criteria of accessibility, availability, and approachability are the most effective qualities to start with when identifying a good mentor, you've taken a major step forward in finding the right mentor.

The people I interviewed for this book are not famous or well-known. I could have taken the angle for this book where I sought out people with a high level of visibility and name recognition to get their thoughts on mentorship. But I believe that mentorship insights from the people I interviewed are much more useful and applicable to you. A friend sent me a message (that they found online) that supports this belief. It goes a little something like this:

Consider the following requests. You don't need to have answers for them; simply think them through and you'll get the point.

1. Name the five wealthiest people in the world.
2. Name the last five Heisman trophy winners.
3. Name ten people who have won the Nobel or Pulitzer Prize.
4. Name the last half-dozen Academy Award winners for best actor and actress.
5. Name the last decade's worth of World Series winners.

These are not second-rate achievers. They are the best in their fields, but they don't have a direct impact on your life. For many of the names you may have come up with, the applause dies, the awards tarnish, and their achievements are merely the answer to a trivia question.

Now think about your answers to this next set of requests.

1. Name five teachers who aided your journey through school.
2. Name five friends who have helped you through a difficult time.

3. Name ten people who have taught you something worthwhile.

4. Name ten people who have made you feel special and appreciated.

5. Name five people you enjoy spending time with.

The lesson here is that the people who make the most difference in your life are not the ones with the most impressive credentials, the most money, or the highest levels of achievements; they are the people who care about you the most.

The participants in my study have a demonstrated history of caring—they built fulfilling relationships and engaged in the mentorship process even when they didn't have to. They continued to invest in those relationships and go through the hard work of mentorship when they could have opted out at any time. In addition to already having easier access to these types of people, these are, in fact, the types of people you should be seeking out to connect with. Building toward a better future requires strong relationships, and strong relationships require people who care about each other. Accolades, accomplishments, fame, and visibility are in no way indicators of the care someone will put into building a relationship with you. Instead, focus on identifying people you can trust to care about you rather than chasing the goal of networking with the biggest names you can find.

Once you have focused your efforts on pursuing mentorship from someone in your network or close to it (either a first- or second-degree connection), consider the relevant subject matter expertise and experience that a mentor must have to provide you with value. If you are just starting your career in a STEM field, you'd benefit from a mentor with a strong technical background. If you identify as part of an underrepresented group within the industry you work, consider a mentor who shares this identity and can provide relevant insights while also helping you with the technical parts of your job. If you are a teenager navigating high school, it makes sense to place a premium on receiving mentorship from someone who grew up in the same town as you and attended the same high school. A deep understanding of your hometown culture and details of the school environment will help the mentor provide you with actionable and realistic advice. Having clarity about your goals, as recommended earlier in this chapter, can help you think of important background characteristics that a potential mentor needs to possess to help you.

A mentee I talked to wanted to develop his public speaking skills while in college. He approached the Pastor at his church, having observed firsthand his subject matter expertise in public speaking. His Pastor not only gave him advice (including life lessons unrelated to public speaking) but also took the mentee to events throughout the summer where he would be speaking to an audience. At these events, the mentee was given the opportunity to learn by watching his mentor in action and then debrief with him afterward. The mentor also would often invite his mentee in front of the audience to tell his story and practice his public speaking. This mentee's life story is admittedly moving and inspirational; in fact, one of his speeches was recorded and went viral. The mentee's college football coaches saw the video (having never heard his story before) and encouraged him to continue sharing his story, both with his teammates as well as the public. Over the years, this mentee has built a successful business as a consultant and motivational speaker. This success originated with a mentor who was not only willing to create time and space for the mentee but was a subject matter expert and had the experience the mentee coveted.

After filtering potential mentors down to people who are available, accessible, approachable, and who possess the relevant subject matter expertise, you can focus on the next step of identifying the right mentor: evaluating the core values and communication style of the potential mentor. Once you've done this, you can determine whether there is enough alignment between these aspects of their personality and your preferred approach to action. You might be surprised at how many people in your network possess a high level of subject matter expertise and are easy to get in touch with. It's an entirely different story, though, when it comes to the people who meet those criteria and also do things "the right way" (or, at the very least, in a way that you would feel comfortable adopting). To be clear, I am not advocating that you find someone who is similar to you in every way. In fact, it's important that your mentor differs from you in some important ways, as those differences create the space for true mentoring and learning to occur. What the research does demonstrate, however, is that your *core values* must be aligned with those of your mentor in order to have the most fulfilling relationship possible.

How can you identify whether the core values and approach of a potential mentor align with your own? As explained earlier in this chapter, you will benefit from both a strong understanding of your own personal values as well as observing your mentor in action to experience how they apply their core values. If you witness consistency over time in how your potential mentor communicates with others and approaches different situations, you can have more confidence in their ability to provide you with the mentorship you need to achieve your goals.

Another mentee I interviewed for this book was Chris Spivey. In addition to his position as the Director of Basketball for the Annie Wright Schools, Chris is the Executive Director of the Center for Community Impact for the YMCA of Pierce and Kitsap counties. Chris was awarded the 2019 Mentor of the Year by Tacoma Mayor Victoria Woodards, but I wanted to solicit his perspective and memories from his experiences as a mentee.

In fact, Chris is the AAU basketball coach I described earlier in the book who observed his mentor intently, made his own sense of surface-level tactics through observation, and was able to focus his conversations with his mentor on program-level strategy topics. Chris mentioned to me that the turning point of the relationship came during a travel tournament in Las Vegas. In travel basketball tournaments, the coaching staff almost always spends time together to plan for the games, chaperone the players, eat meals, etc. As a result of this, Chris was able to observe the consistency of his mentor not just in terms of his demeanor on the sidelines during practice and games but also in how he treated people in the service industry (hotel staff, employees at restaurants, event staff at the games, etc.).

"In situations like that tournament, there's nowhere for you to hide," Chris said. "I saw that this wasn't just who my mentor is as a basketball coach. This is who he is as a person. I always knew I liked and respected him, but the ability to witness his consistency across a ton of different people over a week really confirmed it for me. That spoke to something more than just how he carried himself; it spoke to his values. It spoke to his integrity and his character. Those are things that travel with you 100 percent of the time. Those are the things that really drive a relationship with someone. People can say these are their values, but there's no substitute for seeing someone live those values out and act on them consistently."

This doesn't apply to just basketball. Find opportunities to observe how your potential mentor communicates with others. Be intentional about noticing whether they are consistent in the way they treat others, or if it's dependent on the power dynamic present in the interactions. In addition to observing how your potential mentor communicates, find occasions in which you can witness their decision-making processes, as their methods can give you some insight into their core values.

Another way to evaluate the quality of a potential mentor is to collect data in indirect ways. For example, if people from different departments or divisions at work make time to attend a person's birthday party or baby shower, this can be taken as a signal that this person makes a good impression and is liked by others, regardless of how closely they are connected. Or if you witness people at community events or social gatherings speaking highly of someone when they are brought up in conversation organically, you can be more confident in that person's ability to have a positive impact on your life via mentorship.

In addition to the findings provided in this chapter I recommend you pay close attention to Chapter 9 (Qualities of Good Mentors). If you can observe and experience a person demonstrating the characteristics outlined in Chapter 9, there is a good chance they are the right mentor for you. The research highlights a handful of best practices that are specific to identifying the right mentor for professional mentorship versus personal-life mentorship.

Professional mentorship: The ideal mentors for project-specific and general career trajectory mentorship tend to be people who work in the same organization as the mentee and are as close to the current team/role of the mentee as possible. While the first choice for a mentor should be someone on the same team as you, mentors who partner with mentees in cross-functional roles, or former team members who have left for an internal transfer can also provide a high level of mentorship. Ideal professional mentors possess a balance between having strong institutional knowledge through a long tenure and not being so far removed from the work experience level of the mentee that they struggle to remember what it is like to be less experienced. The best professional mentors, in addition to having experience in the same type of role as the mentee, tend to have between two and eight years more experience on the job than the mentee.

Personal-life mentorship: Demonstrated subject matter expertise in the areas for which you have goals (marriage, having children, making sense of a spiritual journey, etc.) is a critical component to look for when identifying personal-life mentors. This applied understanding and expertise can come from the mentors having already had life experiences in the areas you are interested in, or perhaps they are currently going through the same experiences as you. An important action for a personal-life mentor to merge with their subject matter expertise is to create a shared space for both parties to share honest thoughts and feelings and be vulnerable. Comfort and trust are central to an effective mentor-mentee relationship that focuses on personal life guidance. This is usually built through a shared understanding of experiences. Personal-life mentors are typically easier to identify and develop relationships with than professional mentors.

As I said in the beginning of this chapter, the Preparation stage encompasses all the behind-the-scenes work you should commit to *before* actively pursuing guidance from a mentor. All good construction projects start with a blueprint of what is to be built; in the same way, you should prepare a blueprint for a potential mentorship relationship by taking the necessary steps to better know yourself and what you are looking for in a mentor.

CHAPTER 3

POTENTIAL

Mentors have the dual responsibility of respecting who their mentees currently are while also speaking to the person they can become. As a mentee who is approaching your role with intention, engaging in the first stage of Preparation will help your mentor see where you are in your personal development. Now, in order for mentors to speak to who you can evolve into, it's time to move to the second stage of the process: demonstrating your *potential*.

In the Potential phase of the relationship-building process, you'll move from the behind-the-scenes work of the Preparation stage to taking demonstrable, visible, and tangible actions that highlight your capacity for growth and success in the future. You will also make it clear to your mentor that they can play an impactful role in your development if they are willing to build a relationship with you. This chapter will provide a framework of three ways in which you can display your potential: Observation, Conversation, and Application.

OBSERVATION

I explained in the opening section of the book the value of finding opportunities to *observe* your mentor in action, and in Chapter 2, I recommended using the power of observation to evaluate any alignment between your core values and those of a prospective mentor. The research underscores that receiving mentorship is less about conversations, questions, and answers than you may think. Much of the value from the relationship comes from your engagement and commitment to intentionally listening to and observing your mentor in action.

Several mentees across different types of mentorship relationships spoke to the importance of being able to experience their mentors' behaviors firsthand. A young lawyer told me about the importance of observing his mentor, a more experienced lawyer, in court. "Her command of the courtroom was something I never would have been able to pick up by just talking to her," he told me. "I'm sure she would have explained important parts of how to carry myself during a court appearance, but there are certain nuances that you need to see in order to be able to fully understand. It's something that's hard to put into words. If she had just talked about it with me, I think I would have understood it, but I definitely don't think I would have *gotten it* the way I did when I was able to observe firsthand how she carried herself in the courtroom."

The value of witnessing how mentors carry themselves popped up regularly in my interviews. Another mentee went to her mentor's house for dinner throughout college. "Something that played a huge role in knowing she was the right mentor for me, and for us developing the close relationship we now share, was the opportunity to experience how she is at home," she told me. "I got to see everything. I saw her on her best days and I also saw how she dealt with challenges. Some nights, the dog would be going crazy, or she'd be making dinner and realize she didn't have a couple of ingredients she needed for the recipe, or her kids would need something that came up last minute. It was authentic, and it was honest.

"I didn't have any illusions that things were absolutely perfect at all times. I saw how she carried herself throughout times of craziness, as well as the times when we'd sit down for a nice, relaxing homecooked meal. I respected the honesty and the fact that she wasn't scared of letting me peek behind the curtain to see what was really there. These are all things that I'll probably have experiences with in my future. It helped to build confidence that she'll be honest with me when she gives me thoughts and perspective. It also helped to see that her actions always aligned with the values that she held close to her. I might not always do things exactly the same as her, but I know that the core of it is the same, and I know that I can respect and appreciate the way she does things."

While it's important to observe and scout potential mentors, it's also important to remember that, as a mentee, *you* are being constantly observed and evaluated, even if this is not overtly stated by your mentor. Good mentors naturally observe others and make mental notes about one's potential as a mentee. The best ones do this in what appears to be a seamless, unconscious, and natural manner. A number of mentors noted to me that they are always aware of the prospective mentees who show up consistently, arrive on time, are constantly engaged, and behave, interact, and communicate with others in a way that respects the importance of relationships. The practice of keen observation is your preparation put into action, and it is a signal of your potential. Make sure you fully understand the value of observation (both as the person making the observations and the subject whose actions are being observed) when it comes to demonstrating a high level of potential as a mentee.

CONVERSATION

After deliberately observing a potential mentor, you will want to (tactfully) integrate your observations into conversations with them. When you communicate with them, be sure to cite specific actions, behaviors, ways of communicating, and aspects of the mentor's professional and/or personal approach to situations you observed. Emphasize to them that you made note of these approaches as you observed them and make it clear that you respect that style. Taking it one step further, make it clear that you want to learn more about how you can adopt and adapt their style into your own practice. This will send a signal to your mentor that you are not only prepared and have been practicing the right behaviors without their help, but that their guidance and role in your life as a mentor can provide a high level of value as you navigate the path toward achieving your potential.

A critical component of conversations in a mentor-mentee relationship is the ability to ask good questions of your mentor. Asking the right types of questions helps reinforce the idea that you are intelligent, thoughtful, and deliberate. In addition, the right questions will help ensure you receive the information that is most helpful as you move forward in your growth and development. The universe of potential questions is infinite, and the best questions for mentees to ask are obviously unique to each relationship. However, the research I conducted revealed a general framework that can be helpful to keep in mind as you think of the ideal questions to ask your mentor, which can be broadly divided into two categories: *Information Questions* and *Confirmation Questions*. Both are fundamental categories to draw from and ask of your mentor throughout the relationship, depending on the context at the time of the conversation.

Information Questions: You can use Information Questions in situations where you are looking for advice and directives. These questions typically take the form of "What should *I* do in this situation?" Information Questions are useful when you are in an unfamiliar context and have little clarity about what the correct next steps are. In order to navigate a lack of familiarity, you are looking for information from your mentor that will help guide your upcoming decisions. Good mentors will not only provide perspective on what steps they recommend you take but also offer the logic behind *why* they are suggesting you consider these solutions. Don't be hesitant to ask for the rationale behind their advice. A strong understanding of how the person you respect processes information and solves problems will help you make future decisions independently, as you will be able to apply their system and approach to finding solutions. Information Questions tend to be useful in professional mentorship, particularly early in the relationship when you will be asking about the technical aspects of specific projects.

Confirmation Questions: These questions turn the tables and usually sound something like "What do *you* do in these situations?"

While Information Questions are predicated on receiving advice and solutions for what is best for you, Confirmation Questions ask your mentor to provide anecdotes about their experiences that can provide you with perspective from which you can learn. Confirmation Questions work best in contexts in which you have a level of confidence that you can navigate the situation yourself but would appreciate the perspective of your mentor as you approach your decisions. The anecdotes, stories, and perspectives regarding what your mentor does (or would do) in a similar situation may serve to confirm your plans on how to approach the situation. In the event that your mentor would act differently than you are planning to, you can use their different approach to more clearly understand their perspective and refine your approach.

Confirmation Questions are typically more valuable in personal-life mentorship. For example, if you are a new parent, you might ask one of your personal mentors (who you think is a good parent on the basis of your observations) about how they got their baby on a sleep schedule that worked for the entire family. There are countless books on this topic, and you probably have confidence that you can figure out a solution to this situation yourself. However, taking the step to use Confirmation Questions in conversations with a trusted personal mentor can provide you with valuable insights and considerations as you move forward with your actions.

The finding from the research of Information Questions versus Confirmation Questions provides an example of the distinctions that typify conversations in professional mentorship versus personal-life mentorship. The following considerations should be taken into account when weighing the two distinct types of conversations you might have with your mentor.

Professional conversations: There is usually a pattern to the development of professional mentorship conversations. Early in the relationship, you can expect more of the value from your mentor to come from insights related to technical, logistical, and operational details of projects that you work on. This is the case for two reasons: (1) these areas generally have the steepest learning curves for success when you are an inexperienced mentee in a new organization or role, and (2) receiving technical mentorship early in the relationship gives you the opportunity to assess the subject matter expertise, institutional knowledge, and communication style of your mentor, which helps to inform how to strategically approach future conversations with them. As you progress in your relationship, with a baseline level of comfort, trust, and confidence established by both parties, the topics of conversation start to include big-picture concepts such as general career trajectory and goals. You might also find that you and your mentor start to build a personal relationship. This personal relationship usually helps to accelerate the already promising professional mentorship you are receiving.

Professional mentorship relationships tend to be more successful when the mentee takes the lead on the technical aspects of the relationship (logistics of where and when to meet, an informal heads-up of topics to discuss during the meeting, etc.). While great mentors will be understanding and willing to take on these roles (particularly if you are a young and/or inexperienced mentee), don't forget that *you* are the one receiving advice and value from the mentor. You can build trust and confidence with your mentor by taking the technical pieces of the relationship off their plates (or, at the very least, developing the skills to do so as quickly as possible). A focal point of your role as a mentee in a professional mentorship relationship is to make it as easy as you can for the mentor to be a part of this relationship. Be curious, assertive, and express your needs and desires to the best of your ability so that your mentor knows what their role is and can apply their expertise in the ways that are most beneficial. Essentially, take steps to be the mentee that you would want to have if you were serving as a mentor.

Personal-life conversations: There are obviously fewer best practices learned from the research about how to navigate personal-life mentorship conversations—after all, this should already feel natural and organic. You will likely have a good idea of the role a personal-life mentor can play in your life and the value/perspective they can add. And as a result, you have a good sense—whether you understand why or not—of how to approach conversations with them. Keep in mind that you can still take intentional steps to cultivate a relationship with your personal-life mentor and make the conversations even easier. Be actively involved in events that your mentor hosts; don't simply attend a dinner party they organize, but look for ways in which you can help set up the event, or even offer to help them cook dinner. This will send a signal of care and active involvement as well as give you more opportunities to have one-on-one conversations and share experiences with your mentor.

A final piece for this section is about the importance of *consistent* conversation. Keeping in touch with your mentor helps drive the relationship forward, particularly when you want to move from a transactional relationship and build a transformational relationship. This section outlined categories for the types of questions you can ask your mentor and the best practices for professional mentorship conversations versus personal mentorship conversations, but don't shy away from checking in with your mentor from time to time just to catch up.

Randy Novak, a mentee I interviewed, identified Pamela Smith and Bob Zellner as a pair of mentors for my research project. Pamela enjoyed a career in several caretaker roles (Founder of a doula service company, Medical Aide, Midwife Assistant, and Nurse's Aide) before transitioning to her current role as a Human Rights Activist and Social Justice Consultant. Pamela's current work includes leading civil rights history tours throughout the South, training youth leaders in non-violent direct action, and instructing companies on the beneficial business applications of equality and diversity. Her husband Bob was the first White Field Secretary of the Student Non-Violent Coordinating Committee (SNCC), one of the leading organizations in the civil rights movement of the 1960s, and has been credited with breaking down both institutional and psychological barriers impeding the empowerment of African-American communities. Bob worked alongside many civil rights leaders, most notably Ella Baker, Dr. Martin Luther King Jr., John Lewis, and Rosa Parks.

Randy told me that in the few years since they connected, he has made it a point to speak with his mentors at least two times per week. I asked both Pamela and Bob their thoughts on the importance of Randy's commitment to consistent conversation. "We love talking to him as often as we do," Pamela began, "because he's so open and receptive. He's just a tremendous listener. Quite honestly, I feel like Randy keeps us relevant. I really appreciate the fact that he's so committed to keeping in touch with us. When we talk, there's a mix in the topics of conversation. Sometimes we have an agenda of topics to get through because we partner on work together, but sometimes there are other general topics that he asks our thoughts on."

"The consistency of conversation and discussion helps us get to know each other better," Bob added. "The relationship is the bedrock of our mentorship. No matter how closely aligned you are in your philosophy and organizational approach, you are eventually going to have disagreements. Once you get to the disagreement phase, you can handle that much better if you have a strong personal relationship. That happened in SNCC; we had incredible ripping disagreements! Today, we still have some scars from those disagreements, but we can continue to work together, because before those disagreements we had an incredibly fierce connection to each other based on love, appreciation, and admiration of each other."

"The consistency in our conversations means a lot to me," Pamela noted, "but as Bob said, the transformational piece of our relationship with Randy is the primary thing for me. That connection, friendship, and respect that we have for each other—that's the driving force for me. The transactional aspects of conversation and relationship are necessary, as is the structure that comes with it, but without that transformational piece you don't get the true mentorship relationships that I think people look for."

Another pair Randy identified as important mentors in his life are Renee and Klara Firestone. Renee is a 97-year-old Holocaust survivor. She came to Los Angeles from Czechoslovakia in 1948 following her imprisonment in the infamous concentration camp Auschwitz. Once in Los Angeles, she established a career as a world-famous fashion designer. After starting her own fashion design business in 1960, she experienced a high level of success for nearly two decades. In 1977, Renee began speaking to schools and organizations about the Holocaust. Her compelling story and the value for audiences to hear her unique way of finding meaning in her experience in arguably the darkest period in world history exponentially increased the demand for her speaking engagements. Renee decided to leave her fashion design business and speak full time to ensure that her memories and experiences from the Holocaust would not be lost.

Renee's daughter Klara is named after her sister, who was murdered in the Holocaust. The younger Klara had a successful career as a paralegal for more than three decades before completing her master's degree in clinical psychology with a focus on treating the children of Holocaust survivors. Throughout her life, Klara has followed the lead of her parents and devoted the majority of her time to community service, focusing on social justice issues.

Randy Novak is the founder of Shirts Across America, a non-profit focused on educating high school students about civil rights and social justice issues. Because their pursuits were on parallel tracks, he was able to connect with both Renee and Klara more than a decade ago on a much deeper level. In this time, he has taken intentional steps to ensure that he builds a close relationship with them both.

"I talk to both Renee and Klara a couple of times a week," he began. "I call them every Sunday, at minimum. Before the pandemic, I would get on a flight from Seattle to Los Angeles so I could see them both in person about once a month. It's been like that for a while. Their friendship and mentorship mean a lot to me. The relationship means a lot to me. I definitely keep some things in mind that they tell me that help with decisions about the nonprofit, and I get a ton of perspective from hearing their thoughts. But I just really care about valuing the relationship we've built.

"I've been in Renee's home in Los Angeles many times. Usually while I'm there, the phone will ring a lot—I mean, a lot of people want to talk to Renee and Klara. Renee's story and experiences from the Holocaust are powerful and moving. A lot of people know her and her daughter and want them to speak at different events. But as Renee's gotten older, the phone rings less often. I guess that's because people will reach out to you when they want something, but once you can't do that thing for them anymore, you hear from them less. It's almost like a transaction. As she's gotten older, one thing that's stood out to me is that Renee will end every phone call by saying the same thing: 'Thank you for remembering me.' Well, I want to make sure Renee knows how much I value her. It's a high priority of mine to hear as many of her thoughts as I can while I'm still able to do that. I want to make sure she knows that I will always remember her."

"I prefer that the people around me are not only interesting, but also *interested*," Klara said when asked about the consistency that Randy demonstrates in the relationship. Renee echoed the importance of building a relationship with someone who consistently demonstrates interest in not just maintaining but *growing* the connection. "I have been speaking to an awful lot of schools about my experiences in the Holocaust. You might wonder why I don't have a deeper connection with [more of] the teachers I've met in my time doing this," Renee said. "It's different with Randy. It's because of Randy that this relationship happened. He's the one who followed up with me and continued to be interested in me and my story."

When I relayed Randy's story about the way Renee ends phone calls, she said, "It's funny, because I'm ninety-seven years old now. When I remember somebody that I was friendly with earlier in my life, it gives that person some value because I remember them. I know that with Randy, he will remember me for as long as he lives. I don't know how young people think, but for an old person like me, it means a lot to think that somebody will remember me. It means a lot to me to realize that I won't simply die and disappear. Talking to Randy every week really makes it clear that he remembers me now and will continue to remember me after I'm gone. That makes me feel like, even when I'm gone, I'll still be here through his description of me when he talks to others.

"At this point, just being remembered means so much to me."

Just as Renee said it's important to know that someone remembers her, focus on consistently displaying to your mentor that you are thinking of them and remembering what they have told you.

APPLICATION

When I was young, I was told, "Knowledge is power." But as I've gotten older, I've realized that this phrase is incomplete. Knowledge is actually split into two parts: knowledge *acquisition* and knowledge *application*. The Observation and Conversation aspects of the Potential stage help you to *acquire* knowledge. You pick up tips and tricks from your mentor by observing them, and in response to your questions you get answers and anecdotes that will help you gain new knowledge. But knowledge acquisition by itself doesn't mean anything. In order to truly move forward in achieving your goals and realizing the power that comes with the potential you unlock along that journey, you must engage in knowledge *application*.

Applying the lessons you've learned from your mentor is relatively straightforward. You've done all the behind-the-scenes work to prepare for the relationship. You followed that up with intently observing and intentionally approaching conversations with them in order to learn. Why then, after that entire process, would you stop short of tangibly putting their words into action? One mentor who participated in the research study organizes a successful annual Black and Brown Male Summit with the goal of empowering and motivating young Black and Brown men to excel in both academics and life in general. The event has grown from about twenty-five participants in 2011 to about six hundred young men in more recent years. Throughout his interview with me, the mentor stressed the importance of seeing mentees apply what they've learned from their mentors. While the Black and Brown Male Summit gives these young men the space to learn and be inspired, it is up to each of them to take consistent action and practice what they learned in order to ensure the development of habits that lead to success.

One nuance I will add to this part of the discussion is that, while it is important to apply what you've learned from your mentor, it is essential to be discerning about which pieces of feedback you apply. Good mentors remain open to the idea that not every one of their suggestions throughout the relationship with their mentee will be useful or applicable. These good mentors also have a high level of acceptance that they, even with all their years of experience and subject matter expertise, do not have all the answers and can think about something incorrectly. The level of humility that is practiced by effective mentors means that there needs to be a shared understanding by the mentee that suggestions they receive are not strict directives merely to be acted upon; rather, the feedback and advice mentors provide should be open to discussion, refinement, and even outright rejection.

I interviewed a mentor-mentee pair who were both high school teachers in New York City when they met. "In administrative meetings, we honestly threw a lot at him even though he was a new teacher," the mentor said of his mentee, "because we just had so much work. There was no doubt that he was willing to be a team player and pitch in however he could, but the thing I remember respecting about him was that he was very intentional about the things he would agree to and the things he would push back on. I loved that that was part of his process when the two of us would have meetings. He was always open-minded with what I had to say and the perspective I'd try to provide him with, but he didn't just blindly follow what I said. He put thought into it. I think sometimes there's such a pull when you're receiving mentorship to be the person who signs up for everything and knocks a bunch of different things out of the park. But I think there's way more value in someone who has a good sense of the things they are willing to sign up for and move forward with, the things they are willing to consider with some level of modification, and the things they don't think will work for them."

If you believe that a piece of advice or feedback may not be right for your situation, do your best to voice that to your mentor in a reasonable timeframe. However, don't feel pressured to respond immediately. Mentors will generally be understanding of your need to reflect on their suggestions, internalize them, and make your own sense and meaning of their feedback. Far more important than quickly voicing trepidation in response to an idea put forth by your mentor is having a clear idea of the logic behind *why* you think a suggestion may not work for you. It is better to spend some time considering if your rationale makes sense and how to communicate it effectively than to simply provide an immediate response. Spend the necessary time to reflect on why you don't feel pulled to act on a piece of advice from your mentor and then be sure to communicate those reasons clearly and close the loop on that part of the discussion.

For the advice that you do decide to apply, make sure you reach out to your mentor and provide them with updates of the steps you took, where you are in the process, any results that have come about from your actions, and what your feelings are as you reflect on having applied their suggestions. Being committed to looping back to your mentor and updating them on how you are applying what you learn helps move future conversations forward and keeps your mentor motivated to continue building a relationship with you. They will be more driven to invest time and energy when they see or hear that you are taking actions as a result of your interactions and conversations with them.

Earlier in the book I described a pair of interviewees who worked as administrators at an Ivy League university and would frequent the same on-campus café for their meetings. The mentor in this relationship described the importance of mentees looping back to mentors. "It's important for me to hear not just what works from the people I mentor but what doesn't work," she told me. "Mentees might be a little nervous to communicate the latter, but they should try to keep in mind that there's value, in many ways, for mentors to receive feedback about what doesn't work. First, mentors can take that into account for future meetings and future recommendations they may provide.

"Second, as much as I may be the mentor in our relationship, I can still learn from my mentees. Their perspective and their voice can add to how I think about life. Maybe I'm missing something in terms of how I'm thinking about things. It can also help to inform how I approach other [or future] mentees in my life. That's definitely the case if I provide a resource for one of my mentees and they come back to me and explain why it wasn't helpful. I'll think twice about suggesting that resource for students I work with or people I provide mentorship for if I hear that it isn't as effective of a tool as I thought it was."

Above all, mentors want your honest assessment of how effective their suggestions have been as you continue to apply them. Your mentor wants to know whether the thoughts they offered or the resources they provided were useful. Don't be afraid to tell them if you applied something they suggested or utilized a resource they provided and you didn't find it helpful. The types of mentors that you want to keep in your life will want to learn more about why some of their suggestions aren't helpful. They'll consider your perspective and how it might inform their approach to their own lives and adjust their recommendations in the future—not only to you, but also to other mentees they may be serving.

CHAPTER 4
PROGRESS

The last stage of intentionally approaching your role as a mentee involves demonstrating your *progress*. This phase of development builds from the foundation you establish in the Preparation stage and the actions you take in the Potential stage to drive your continuous growth. Parts of this chapter will call back to insights provided in Chapter 3 (Potential), as the Progress stage is essentially your ability to *consistently* demonstrate your potential.

This chapter will outline a framework to use when planning for and later evaluating the progression of the relationship with your mentor. Two separate frameworks will be presented: one for professional mentorship and one for personal-life mentorship. The professional mentorship framework includes estimates of how long each phase of the progression should take as you build the relationship. (It's important to note that these time estimates are for *in-person* contact with your professional mentor. While I can't provide timeframe guidelines for the virtual interactions that are more common as a result of the pandemic, I am confident that each of these phases will require more time virtually than in-person.) These frameworks are based on the patterns and trends that emerged from the responses provided by the interviewees.

PROFESSIONAL MENTORSHIP PROGRESSION FRAMEWORK

Phase 1: The first of the five phases of professional mentorship places an emphasis on your commitment to practicing observation. Phase 1 also includes the transition from observation to the initial stages of conversation with your professional mentor. These early conversations will involve technical questions (typically Information Questions) about specific projects you have. They also can include general queries about how to approach project management, such as, "How do I figure out which projects should be at the top of my priority list?" Throughout Phase 1, you are gaining tangible feedback, perspective, and advice from your mentor on how to be successful in your job. Through this input, you are creating the opportunity to evaluate the chemistry with your mentor on the basis of their communication style and how their recommendations intersect with your preferred methods of approaching your work. The Phase 1 steps of observation, initial conversations, and evaluating the dynamic with your professional mentor typically takes between thirty and fifty hours of contact time over the course of a month-and-a-half to two months.

Phase 2: After the initial two months of absorbing information, you can move into Phase 2 of your professional mentorship relationship by proactively anticipating the types of questions your mentor will ask you and the feedback they will provide. To do this, you must reflect on your conversations with your professional mentor from both formal and informal meetings and make sense of their process to come up with answers, thoughts, and responses to your questions. The biggest difference between phases 1 and 2 is that you are focused on asking good Information Questions and executing on the recommendations made by your mentor in Phase 1; in Phase 2, rather than simply asking Information Questions, you will come prepared with ideas on how to move forward by proactively thinking of the feedback your mentor is likely to provide.

The options you voice to your mentor as paths to move forward don't have to be well thought out or in-depth. The potential courses of action you voice are a signal to your mentor that you are starting your own critical thinking process and bringing the seeds of ideas to the table. Phase 2 will involve a high level of learning, and consequently a high level of failure. Several of your initial thoughts are likely to be rejected. But be sure to take the feedback in the right spirit and as an opportunity to refine your problem-solving processes rather than feel like you are not cut out for the job. (Balancing your emotions when receiving critical feedback is made easier by having a good mentor who is skilled at approaching this communication in a tactful manner.) In addition to refining your system and approach to problem solving, Phase 2 also will provide you with the opportunity to redefine the ways you are looking at the challenges you are facing and the questions you are bringing to your mentor.

These Phase 2 conversations occur one or two times per week for about four months. You can expect each of these conversations to be about an hour long. Do your best to keep Phase 2 conversations as informal as possible (if your professional mentor has an "open-door policy," now is the time to use it). These four months are also the appropriate timeframe in which to start building a personal rapport with your professional mentor, such as by asking about family and friends. This not only helps keep Phase 2 conversations more informal but will also help you and your mentor connect more easily in professional conversations in the upcoming phases of your relationship.

Phase 3: After the first six months of your professional relationship with your mentor, you can move from asking Information Questions to asking Confirmation Questions in your conversations. Building on the vague, introductory ideas of paths to take you offered in Phase 2, Phase 3 marks a shift in your approach as you focus on devising your own in-depth idea and plan (we can codify this as developing your own *strategy*). Your strategy is not based on thoughts off the top of your head; rather, it's the culmination of intentional reflection, processing, and problem solving.

In Phase 3, you are coming to your professional mentor with detailed thoughts of how to move forward, organized in a unified, cogent manner. Upon presenting your proposed strategy to your mentor, you can ask Confirmation Questions that will help you receive their feedback, considerations, and perspective. In this phase of your relationship, your mentor still plays a large role as someone you are proactively seeking out for feedback. However, the nature of their feedback is different. Instead of playing a central role in creating and driving your plans, they now act as a sounding board who "rounds out the edges" of your ideas and adds considerations that you can use to refine your strategic approach to your projects and overall work.

The conversations in Phase 3 still occur one or two times per week on average and are still about an hour long. Phase 3 lasts for about six months (at this point, your mentorship relationship will have progressed through three phases over the course of a year). In cases where a relationship has progressed organically (rather than beginning with a formal discussion about receiving mentorship), the end of Phase 3 is around the time that both mentees and mentors begin to feel that a mentorship relationship has been established.

Phase 4: After about a year of a strong working relationship with your mentor, you can start asking for thoughts on the strategic direction of your career (how to prepare for a promotion, navigate conversations about a raise, general career considerations, etc.). If your initial goal in receiving professional mentorship was to navigate your overall career trajectory and intentionally work toward a big career event such as a promotion, you can certainly progress to Phase 4 in less than a year. However, don't forget that it's difficult to expedite the ability of your mentor to provide you with valuable, customized, targeted feedback that is best for you; they must observe your discipline, approach, and thought process to your work *consistently* over a long period of time.

One reason it takes at least a year to dive into meaningful conversations about career trajectory is that you need to have had enough time in your role to fully understand the day-to-day demands of doing your job well. Additionally, there need to have been ample opportunities for you to observe your mentor in action. An interviewee who currently works for Boston Consulting Group told me that he needed at least a year in a previous consultant role to have a complete understanding of the demands of the role and how to approach client meetings. He was able to pick up little nuances from his mentor on conference calls and client meetings throughout the course of the year and was able to adopt and adapt them into his own work with clients.

The estimate of one year on the job to reach full productivity certainly isn't specific to technology consulting. A lawyer I interviewed told me that she thinks it takes twelve to eighteen months minimum for a lawyer fresh out of law school to be able to do their work independently. She noted that even established professionals with decades of experience have a steep learning curve when they start a job at a new firm or government agency. Keep this in mind as you navigate broader conversations about your career trajectory. Don't forget that part of your responsibility as a mentee is to focus on today before tomorrow. Rather than rush to get the next promotion and enjoy upward mobility in your career, make sure that you are focused on practicing the behaviors that set the foundation for being successful in your current role. This will require time, patience, and commitment on your part.

The goal of mentorship is to cultivate a meaningful relationship with another person—and there are no shortcuts. The best mentees (as well as mentors) commit to developing a deep relationship with the right person, and trust that the rest will fall into place and goals will be achieved. The timelines related to Phase 4 vary much more than the timeframes for the first three phases owing to the adaptive nature of general career trajectory questions (especially when compared to the technical nature of project-specific questions in the first three phases). You can spend as much time in Phase 4 discussions as your mentor will give you. Just be sure to keep the lessons from Chapter 3 in mind as you navigate an appropriate timeframe for Phase 4 conversations, particularly around the value of *applying* the feedback your mentor provides.

Phase 5: The final phase of a professional mentorship relationship is one in which you as the mentee are now able to openly discuss work ideas with your mentor and provide *them* with value and perspective. Essentially, you are able to serve your mentor in some of the same capacities they have served you throughout your relationship. In this phase, you are also able to discuss big-picture career options for which your mentor might want your input. A lot of mentees feel uncomfortable in the initial shift to Phase 5. This is a common feeling, but the research shows that if you push through the initial discomfort, having the space for a reciprocal relationship is ultimately the ideal outcome for both parties.

Earlier in this book, I mentioned my interview with a former Admiral in the US Navy. He told me that he felt like he "had a responsibility to pay back the relationship" to his mentor. This statement perfectly describes Phase 5. At the end of the day, mentors are people too. They go through their own stress and can benefit from a strong support system. Having spent more than a year building a relationship with your professional mentor that has progressed through the first four phases, you have the opportunity (or as the former Admiral viewed it, an obligation) to be a part of your mentor's support system if and when they need to lean on someone for help and perspective.

PERSONAL-LIFE MENTORSHIP PROGRESSION FRAMEWORK

While professional mentorship progresses through chronological phases, the personal-life mentorship progression moves through *levels*. The difference here is that personal-life mentorship is often less goal-oriented than professional mentorship. Timeframes and progression through sequential phases may be important in a professional sense, whereas with *levels*, the most fulfilling type of relationship for a mentor might not necessarily be what you are looking for in your personal life—and that's okay! There is an element of chronology in that you can't get to a higher level without spending at least some time in each of the previous levels. Ultimately, however, the sequence isn't the main focus. Rather, it's simply about creating space for both parties to be at a level that you, as the mentee, desire. As a result, there are no timeframes specified for each level in the personal-life mentorship progression framework. If you want to progress to a higher level, that comes down to a nontechnical, informal decision made jointly by you and your mentor. In Chapter 1, I discussed the difference between a person being a "get to" rather than a "have to." For personal-life mentorship, it's all about focusing on being a "get to" at the level of relationship that is right for you.

Level 1: In the first level, you have a desire for a sense of community in your personal life and are seeking only a surface-level relationship with a mentor (in the context of a broader group). Examples of these interactions include connecting at an event for a spiritual organization, attending a dinner party with family and friends in attendance, or joining a community event with a larger group of fellow students. While you might pick up a couple of useful nuggets from a specific mentor at any of these events, your purpose and intention for attending is to be with a group of people rather than to connect on a deeper level with a specific individual. The mentor can provide value and small pieces of mentorship in a Level 1 context, but it is not targeted and customized for you specifically.

Level 2: In Level 2, you are drawn to a specific individual in a social setting or group (for example, a religious organization or sports team that you are both involved with). It is your responsibility to demonstrate that you would like to pursue a relationship with this potential mentor by seeking out opportunities to interact with them in a one-on-one capacity. An example of this provided in Chapter 3 is to offer to help set up dinner or even cook with the potential mentor if you are invited to a dinner party they are hosting. Taking proactive steps to assist them will go a long way in helping the mentor feel more comfortable with you and will help build their trust in you. Engaging in these steps also gives both you and your potential mentor ample opportunity to assess how you fit with each other.

Level 3: While Level 2 conversations can stay on surface-level topics, even in a one-on-one setting, Level 3 conversations involve opening up to your mentor and displaying a level of vulnerability.

In these interactions, you are simply asking your mentor to listen to you and be present as you make meaning of your deeper thoughts, challenges, or upcoming decisions. Topics of conversation might include looking to make sense of relationship difficulties with others, insecurities about your ability to succeed in your current job, or a general feeling of being lost and having no clear direction for your future. Your mentor in a Level 3 relationship will ask questions to help facilitate your processing of information and encourage you to set aside the requisite time for reflection to make sense of these deeper thoughts and feelings.

Level 4: This step is one in which you—in addition to your mentor being present as you process information—invite your mentor to give their advice and thoughts. Instead of mentors simply making you feel supported by listening and asking questions that may be useful for you as you try to make sense of your given situation, Level 4 involves what most people think of when they consider the topic of mentorship: a mentor giving feedback and recommendations. While the role of mentors in Level 3 can be thought of as passive, mentors in Level 4 take on a more *active* role in helping you process your thoughts about your personal life.

I began my research on mentorship in September 2020. One mentee I interviewed focused part of our conversation on the mentorship he received for approaching his role as a parent. "These past few months, as a result of some really tragic and heartbreaking events, we as a country are starting to have some really difficult conversations around race relations, particularly in terms of the Black experience in America," he began. "I'm the father of two sons who are Black. They've had a lot of questions and there are a lot of important things that I'm committed to educating myself on that, even as a Black man, I wasn't aware of. And as I read more and learn more about the history of Black people in this country and what we've gone through, it honestly is painful. It hurts. It's sad, it's upsetting, it's frustrating, it makes me angry—it's all of that rolled into one.

"But on top of all that, I need to figure out how I bring all this to raising my kids. My mentor is much more educated and well-versed in topics related to Black history and the Black experience than I am. I've called him multiple times these past few months and had conversations about it all. What's amazing about him is that he has such a command of knowing when to listen and let me process all of this for myself. He knows that part of what I need is just someone who can simply be there and ask questions to facilitate my thought process. But it's also my responsibility to get as much value from him as I can. He has kids, and as a Black father of Black kids, he has navigated all of this. So, it's my job to ask him about his experiences with managing his emotions as he learned about all the things I'm learning now. It's my job to give him an invitation to give me advice on how to deal with all these emotions when talking to my kids about what it means to be Black in America, both historically and currently."

Level 5: This level of personal-life mentorship requires you to integrate the final lesson of Chapter 3—*applying* the advice and thoughts your mentor gives you in Level 4. Again, I want to note here that, if you are pursuing personal-life mentorship, you do *not* have to focus on progressing through all of the levels if that is not what you want out of the relationship. In fact, having a collective group of mentors across each level is important to us in our personal lives. Think about the importance of having a range of connections in your life, from acquaintances to close confidants. Each of these groups of people provides value in our lives, and the same holds true for a range of mentors. You do not need to feel obligated to apply all the recommendations a personal-life mentor gives you, particularly when their feedback does not align with your personal values or your preferred approach to doing things. However, if you do decide to engage in Level 5 mentorship and apply some of the thoughts and advice your mentor gives you, be sure to follow up to let them know of the actions you took, the results of these actions, and how you feel about them. This will help continue the momentum of conversation and put you on the trajectory toward Level 6, if that is a goal of yours.

Level 6: This is the personal-life mentorship equivalent of professional mentorship's Phase 5. In Level 6, your mentor-mentee relationship becomes reciprocal. In the context of personal-life mentorship, Level 6 is where both you and your mentor make the relationship a two-way street in which *you* provide your mentor with guidance and value. One of the unique mentor-mentee pairs in the research study started in a professional mentorship capacity that became a close personal friendship over the years. In this relationship, the mentee I interviewed still continues to receive professional mentorship from her mentor. However, because of their close friendship, the mentee is able to provide personal-life mentorship for her mentor. Part of being a mentor is simply to create a safe space for the other person to feel comfortable and supported. In this example, the mentee regularly suggests a hike or a weekend getaway for them to do together. Typically, she suggests these ideas when she observes that her mentor seems stressed at work. By intentionally creating space for her mentor to decompress and reset, the mentee is taking steps similar to those that her mentor has taken over the years (specifically in a work context). As expressed by a number of the interviewees who participated in personal-life mentorship, Level 6 is where both people feel that the other person is not just a friend, but a family member whom they've chosen.

In the Progress stage, you focus on internalizing all that you have learned from your mentor, integrating those lessons into a general system for problem solving, and creating processes for how you approach the future. This stage emphasizes a growth in your attitudes toward engaging with your future. Intentional mentees who have progressed to this final stage have consistently practiced building processes and systems for problem solving over a long period of time, and they move from needing motivation to being disciplined enough to carry out a standardized set of best practices regardless of the challenges they are navigating. This discipline allows you to enjoy opportunities for sustained success in the future, both professionally and personally.

CHAPTER 5
QUALITIES OF GOOD MENTEES

In addition to prescriptive recommendations for how mentees can intentionally approach the Preparation, Potential, and Progress stages of their roles, I want to offer a handful of qualities that great mentors have identified in an ideal mentee. For your convenience, I am separating the qualities of a good mentee into two categories. The first category regards qualities that mentors look for in the early stages of the relationship. After all, you get only one opportunity to make a first impression. The second category is comprised of the qualities that mentors would like to see mentees exemplify once the relationship has been established. Essentially, this category expounds on the behaviors that mentors want to see their mentees practice in order for them to continue investing in the relationship. Keep the findings from this chapter in mind to inform the lens through which you view your responsibilities as a mentee during the relationship-building process with your mentor.

QUALITIES OF GOOD MENTEES IN THE INITIAL STAGES OF MENTORSHIP

The 3 Es: As a mentee, you can control three Es: excitement, enthusiasm, and energy. Be *excited* about the prospect of building a genuine relationship with someone you can learn from. And even if you are naturally more laid back, you can still demonstrate *enthusiasm* to your mentor in every interaction you have with them regarding where you are in your life, the potential for your future, and the relationship you can build with your mentor along the way. (For those of you who are naturally enthusiastic, be sure that your enthusiasm doesn't go past a productive range and become *excessive exuberance*.) While there are certainly things about life that you can't control, one of the few things you always have full power over is your choice to be an *energy giver* (rather than an energy sucker).

I had the opportunity to interview Jeremy Mills, host of the Jeremy Mills Podcast, as one of the mentees in the research study that informed this book. Jeremy's mentor is Jamal Crawford, who has played for nine teams over the course of his twenty-year NBA career. Jamal organizes an annual summer Pro-Am called The CrawsOver in his hometown of Seattle. Admission to The CrawsOver is free for the general public in the basketball-crazy city. Past guests have included Blake Griffin, Kevin Durant, and Kobe Bryant. Jeremy, drawn to watching high-level basketball games, was able to build a relationship with Jamal. The trust and confidence in the relationship grew to the point where Jamal chose Jeremy to run the podcast affiliated with The CrawsOver.

Jamal has spoken publicly about the fact that many people approached him and expressed an interest in being the point-person for a CrawsOver podcast. He has also explained in interviews why he felt that Jeremy was the right person for such a high-profile position. In addition to possessing characteristics explained previously in this book (such as consistency and being great in his current role), Jeremy carried himself at The CrawsOver in a way that lent itself to Jamal being able to take notice of Jeremy's potential.

As I listened to an interview Jeremy conducted with Jamal, asking him why he decided Jeremy was the right host for the CrawsOver podcast, I was struck by Jamal complimenting Jeremy's excitement, enthusiasm, and energy every time he saw him. Jeremy's commitment to the three Es got him noticed by a twenty-year NBA veteran who does amazing things both on and off the court. Demonstrating behaviors related to the three Es went a long way in having Jamal view Jeremy as a "get to" type of person. While Jamal only texted out quotes to the media while he was in the 2020 NBA Bubble, he made the time to give an interview on the Jeremy Mills Podcast. As you think about your approach to being more intentional as a mentee, commit to displaying excitement, demonstrating enthusiasm, and delivering energy.

Curiosity: The vast majority of mentors I interviewed specified the value of a growth and learning mindset in their mentees when they start the mentorship process. Be interested and open to doing things in a new way. One of the foundational components of a mentorship relationship is the opportunity to learn new perspectives and approaches to improve your effectiveness. True learning and growth never occur in easy contexts, so make sure you develop the capacity to "be comfortable with feeling uncomfortable." It is critical for you to be receptive and open to feedback, particularly thoughts and advice that necessitate you change in order to improve.

"One of the best things you can do [as a mentee] is follow your curiosity," said the Google employee I interviewed. "I think it's important to know what you are open to and to be excited and curious about those things. You should constantly assess your job, life, skills, and goals. I think it's also important to make sure that you have a range of experiences so that you have a sense of what's out there. At the end of the day, I think what matters is being open to learning new things. It's easier to learn new things when you know what you want to learn, and that can't happen if you aren't curious about what's out there."

The mentors I interviewed seemed to notice a pattern in which mentees who demonstrated high levels of curiosity and a learning/growth mindset also tended to have a higher capacity for humility. A high level of humility allows mentees to take constructive feedback in good spirits. A handful of mentees I interviewed admitted that they tend to be emotional when receiving uncomfortable feedback. A tip they suggested is to take notes when receiving recommendations about what you need to change. By focusing on the technical task of notetaking, you might be able to be less emotional and minimize visceral reactions to hearing advice that you might struggle with at first. A key second step after expressing curiosity is to practice reflection and introspection. Make sense and meaning of conversations with your mentor, as well as experiences outside of the relationship that you can communicate to your mentor if you would like their thoughts.

Share about yourself: Good mentors will try to do what is best for *you*. In order for them to give advice and feedback that is unique to you, they need to know enough about you—your values, your preferred methods, your areas of comfort, where you draw your confidence from, etc. You can expedite this process by sharing more about yourself. Authenticity is key to this aspect of being a good mentee. Don't give the answers you think your mentor wants to hear or that portray you in the best light. Rather, be tactful and respectful while also being true to yourself and honest about yourself.

I had the opportunity to interview an entrepreneur who founded a boutique music, entertainment, and brand development company. Thanks to his successful career that has included international tours, record deals, TV appearances, and a long-standing multimedia campaign partnership with Starbucks, this individual has been approached by a number of people seeking mentorship. "In terms of conversations I have with people I might mentor," he said, "I try to be a great listener and ask the questions that are worthwhile. I challenge my mentees and see if they step up to the plate to confront these challenges. It's kind of like the 'bob and weave' in boxing. As a mentor, I try to be patient as I listen to my mentees throw everything at me. I'm bobbing and weaving as they send all the information my way, allowing it to come at me but careful not to get caught up in it. I just keep my eyes on the bigger picture while they give me the information.

"Then there's a certain point when I pop them with a suggestion or piece of feedback. I throw it back on them. That's where I think a lot of value comes from. But all of this is predicated on me knowing my mentees. Before I get to a place where I can provide them with value, I need to know them as a person. That's made easiest when they're willing to be open and share details about themselves. Then I know exactly how to make sense of what they're saying as I 'bob and weave.' I know exactly what the bigger picture is. I have a good idea of what to throw at them that would be best for them. They need to set the foundation for the relationship by being willing to tell me as much as they can about themselves."

On a personal level, I am a very private and guarded person, so this quality of being a good mentee isn't easy for me. However, I can't argue the patterns in responses that came up in the research interviews. Being a good mentee requires some degree of vulnerability that comes with communicating openly about yourself. With trust being such a key component of a deep, genuine relationship with a mentor, I must be better about demonstrating that I trust potential mentors by opening up more than I typically do.

Thoughtfully quiet: In Part II, I provided insights about having conversations with your mentor: how to ask better questions, demonstrate curiosity, and open up more about yourself. In addition to being skilled in these areas, mentors that I interviewed stressed the importance of mentees thinking of communication and conversations in terms other than actively speaking. Along the lines of being a keen observer, you can send signals to your mentor that you are thinking about situations without having to speak. In the times that you do speak, it can carry more weight since there is an indication that you speak less frequently to put in real thought during times of silence. Some ways to be intentional about being thoughtfully quiet include showing up on time, showing up consistently, and being engaged/fully present at all times (focusing on the meeting at hand or observing what is happening rather than being on your phone or computer, etc.).

Work ethic meets ambition: This quality reflects your understanding as a mentee of what it means to *consistently* work hard over a long period of time. Mentors value mentees who understand that being smart and a hard worker does not guarantee that you will achieve your goals. Mentors told me stories of prospective mentees throughout the years who had accurate views of their potential; however, in communicating their ambitions, these mentees seemed to imply that achieving their goals was a foregone conclusion because they "deserve it." While they certainly may deserve those future successes, the mentors stated that the best mentees have a strong understanding that life does not always result in achieving what you "deserve." They want mentees who fully understand what it means to earn those future outcomes and stick with the right behaviors, rather than think they are guaranteed results.

Jeremy Mills is a great example of a mentee who lives out the trait of work ethic meeting ambition. His path to hosting the official podcast for The CrawsOver looks something like this: years of journalism experience throughout high school; hosting and producing about 150 episodes of the Jeremy Mills Podcast before "having a clear idea of what the voice and angle of the podcast should be"; years of attending The CrawsOver and slowly building a relationship with Jamal Crawford by attending each game and standing in line for a picture with or autograph from Jamal. After setting this foundation, it still takes multiple hours—across multiple days—to research each podcast guest in preparation for the interview.

"There's a whole lot of preparation that goes into it, and nothing is guaranteed," Jeremy told me. "Jamal was awesome at connecting me with amazing people, vouching for me, and encouraging people to let me interview them. But sometimes the interview just doesn't happen for whatever reason. Either something comes up last minute for one of the players or they just don't have the time. But I still have to be ready, just in case they actually *are* available for an interview. I think that's something that's really important: being prepared for an opportunity that likely won't happen.

"It really is a full-time job to prepare correctly, and I get why it might be frustrating for some people to put in all that effort and not get the opportunity they were preparing for, but I think that's just the definition of hard work. Even when what you want isn't guaranteed—or even isn't likely to happen—you still do all the right things anyway. At the very least, I got in reps and practice, which probably made me better in the interviews that *did* wind up happening. I just think it's better to be confident that you're ready for an opportunity that winds up happening because you did all the hard work."

Express gratitude: Every mentor I spoke to made it clear that they do not undertake the responsibilities of being a mentor to receive appreciation, nor is it something that they expect as part of the relationship. However, they all stated that they always treasure the kind words whenever gratitude is expressed by their mentee. Outside of practicing mentorship, your mentor has their own life with their own family, their own work, their own responsibilities, and their own challenges. Don't forget that mentors are people too! Being appreciative of the work they have put in on your behalf goes a long way in supporting their mental and emotional health. Not hearing appreciation and gratitude can have a negative effect on them. You may not be able to influence other people in your mentor's life to express appreciation and love, but you can control your own response to your mentor. Make it a point to thank them for the specific ways in which you appreciate their involvement in your growth and development—and do this consistently. You should express gratitude every step of the way, and you can build the habit right off the bat in the relationship.

QUALITIES OF GOOD MENTEES AS THE MENTORSHIP RELATIONSHIP PROGRESSES

Application of feedback: This has been a consistent theme throughout this book. As I said in Chapter 3, mentors like to see mentees act on at least some of the feedback that is provided. An important piece of applying the recommendations made by your mentor is to proactively follow up with them. Reach out to them, provide them with details of the actions you took, the results you have seen, and how you feel about it.

Progress in your process: In addition to the details, results, and feelings you have after applying feedback from your mentor, you should demonstrate some progress over time of how you process information and events. An ideal mentee doesn't say yes to everything. Instead, there is a level of discernment you need to have in regard to which requests you say yes to and which aren't aligned with your values or goals. This works best if you can explain the *why* behind your decisions on what to take on and what not to. Explaining your rationale is not a test that you have to pass for your mentor; rather, it is simply a way to have language behind your decisions and to practice effective communication.

Reactive to proactive: When your commitment to applying feedback from your mentor intersects with progress in how you process information, you can demonstrate a shift in *how* you apply the feedback that has been provided. Early in the relationship, you will start by merely executing the advice of your mentor. As the relationship moves forward and you start to improve your decision-making processes under the guidance of your mentor, you can proactively adapt and adopt their problem-solving skills into your own behaviors. If your relationship started as one in which your mentor was initiating meetings (either owing to your youth or inexperience level as a mentee), look to take a more proactive approach in this area as the relationship grows. Over time, develop the conviction, confidence, and assertiveness to handle the logistics of meetings, speak up in different situations, and communicate your thoughts. Ultimately, a good mentor *wants* you to become self-sufficient. A level of self-sufficiency is required as you commit to moving from being reactive and passive in your approach to being proactive.

Drive and discipline: As much as your relationship and many of the behaviors you practice as a mentee will evolve, be sure to keep the same drive and discipline as you had when you began the relationship. Bringing the three Es (excitement, enthusiasm, and energy) is easy in the beginning of any new relationship, but maintaining momentum over a long period of time is difficult. As I've expressed throughout this book, consistency over a long period of time is necessary for a fulfilling mentorship relationship at the highest level. As one of the mentors I talked to said, "I don't want to be in a position where I'm wondering how I evaluated a mentee more highly [in the early stages of] the relationship than as it progressed." Don't get away from the basics that worked for you and put you in a position to be recognized by your mentor as someone they'd like to invest in and create a relationship with. Continue to outwork everyone and have goals that are related to being a positive influence on others.

Reciprocal relationship: Mentors ultimately find the highest level of fulfillment when their mentee gets to a place where they are comfortable enough to return the favor for what the mentor has done for them throughout the relationship. A true two-way street is the ideal outcome for those who engage in the hard work and responsibility of providing mentorship consistently over a long period of time. Reward your mentor by thinking critically about how you might be able to take proactive steps to add value to their lives—these situations often present themselves naturally. As I said earlier, mentors are people too. They hold their own insecurities, doubts, and fears. They, like you, are their own harshest critic. If you take the steps outlined in Part II to be an intentional mentee, you likely will have built enough trust and confidence in the relationship for your mentor to be able to express vulnerability about a situation they are facing. As much as it might be unfamiliar territory within the context of your relationship, be ready to provide for your mentor what they have been giving you throughout your time together. Give them support and encouragement. Challenge them to think differently and view things from a new perspective. Be a trusted confidant who can strike a good balance between what they need to hear and how they want to hear it.

You may have read this book with the purpose of learning more about how to be an intentional mentee because that is the role more applicable to you, but the next section will provide some valuable information as well. Understanding the insights and recommendations for being a more intentional *mentor* can help you, as a mentee, understand more about the responsibility and role of the person you are building a relationship with. You'll also want to be ready for the reciprocal relationship stage with your mentor when that time comes. In addition, you might want to start considering what *your* approach to being a mentor might look like. Mentorship relationships tend to spring up unexpectedly. You just might be the right person to provide mentorship to someone else. If that's the case, you'll want to be ready to intentionally approach that process.

PART III

HOW TO BE AN INTENTIONAL MENTOR

CHAPTER 6

PATIENT PERSISTENCE

A s a mentor, you might think of yourself as someone whose role is to guide your mentee to a better future as quickly as possible. However, that is the second step of your two-part job. First, you need to validate who your mentee currently is. A relationship in which you are solely focused on your mentee's potential for a better future will not inspire the trust and confidence required for a fulfilling relationship. In addition to seeking your help as they navigate their path to a better future, your mentee will also look to you for validation, and to truly validate where your mentee currently is in their life, you must commit to getting to know them over a long period of time.

Although it might seem like understanding who mentees currently are and speaking to who they can be in the future are two distinct responsibilities, a common theme connects these two obligations: your ability to remain *patiently persistent*. There are a number of best practices to incorporate into your relationship with your mentee to be a more intentional mentor, and the prerequisite for these behaviors is the capacity to consistently practice grace and understanding.

It's important to note that, while this entire chapter advises you remain patient with a potential mentee, you must balance this with transparency and honesty as early as possible if you decide there isn't alignment between your background and their intended goals (or in your communication styles and core values). You should remain open to the idea that you might not be the right mentor for the potential mentee for these reasons. However, the research highlights that if you do think there is a good fit, you must be committed to being patiently persistent in your relationship to practice true mentorship.

Make no mistake: practicing patient persistence is not an easy task for mentors to accomplish. It's difficult to remain patient over a long period of time with a mentee, particularly if you feel they might not be putting enough effort into the relationship or taking your guidance to heart. This challenge is compounded by the fact that you are still facing your own stressors and navigating your own life. Great mentors, however, are able to dig deep in these tough times and find ways to remind themselves to remain patient with their mentees and demonstrate that patience persistently throughout the relationship.

I touched upon a framework for mentees to strategically identify a good mentor in Part II, and it deserves a deeper dive here for those reading this book in hopes of becoming more intentional in their practices as a mentor. A pattern of three abilities stands out when identifying what makes a great mentor: *accessibility*, *availability*, and *approachability*. As you move forward in improving your capacities in these areas, keep in mind that patience and persistence over a long period of time are required to be the best mentor possible for your mentee in each of these aspects of the relationship.

ACCESSIBILITY

One of the first hurdles for mentees to clear is simply having *access* to a potential mentor. The sad truth about mentorship is that people who would benefit the most from positive guidance, deep relationships, and a strong presence by a mentor generally have a tougher time accessing them. It's important to keep this in mind and be more intentional about making yourself accessible to those who can benefit from your mentorship. One mentee I interviewed described how her mentor in high school always carved out time for her, whether it was at social gatherings, school, or at church. She is now in her final year of college and finds it just as easy now to have access to her mentor, who always texts or calls her back immediately and is consistently ready to provide her with the support and guidance she is seeking.

Being more accessible requires you to press pause on your value judgments and preconceived notions about a potential mentee until you have had more opportunities to speak with them. While you might pride yourself on being able to read people, quickly assess their potential, and have the life experiences that inform your view of the right way to do things, you must keep in mind that mentorship is all about the mentee. You don't get to choose who can potentially benefit from your time, effort, and guidance. You also don't get to choose how mature and refined their approach is to initiating conversations with you. A pair of interviews I conducted provide powerful examples of the positive outcomes that are possible if you remain patient and accessible.

Dr. John Gaines is a successful entrepreneur, leadership consultant, author, and motivational speaker. One of his mentors is a Pastor he connected with over a decade ago. "I remember the first time I had a meeting with him," he recounted. "I was going into my junior year of college and I knew I wanted to improve my public speaking skills. I had seen him speak before and I knew I could learn from him. I asked him for some time to meet and he was gracious enough to take a meeting with me. Even though I was an adult and knew enough about how to fight and get a seat at the table, I had never really had a lot of people in my life hold me accountable. I hadn't learned some of the lessons that others learn earlier in their lives. I came to the meeting five minutes late.

"My mentor was already sitting down at the coffee shop inside the church. I remember before we started talking, a guy walked by and my mentor waved to him. He then turned to me and said, 'You see that guy? That wave hello is as much time as he'll get from me. I know his first name, but I just don't have a lot of free time to connect in more depth with most people. I choose to give my time to certain groups of people. First is my family, who are really important to me. Second are people I connect with in my profession, namely with work at church. And then third are the people

I mentor in relationships like this one. The reason I do it this way is because time is the one thing you never get back. If you want my time and I'm willing to give you time, don't be late. You can never be late again if you ask for my time.'

"I think a lot of people would have shied away from saying what he said to me or, even worse, dismissed me right off the bat for being late to the meeting because they would have assumed I was being disrespectful," he continued. "But I really appreciated him saying it, especially the way he did. He was firm but polite. He made it clear that he wasn't judging me and that the lines of communication are still open as long as I put his feedback into action. I knew I needed to continue to talk with people like that—people who are strong but practice grace. I shadowed him for the whole summer. I continued to reach out and take advantage of the fact that he was so willing to be accessible. And I learned my lesson about being on time for meetings."

I was intrigued by the anecdote and curious about how his mentor was so understanding in this situation. I'll admit that, if I were in the position of the mentor, I might've taken lateness to our meeting as a sign of disrespect, lack of professionalism, and absence of commitment to the hard work necessary to achieve his goals. I know for a fact that a number of people in my life would have had the same reaction if they were on the receiving end of an adult being late to a meeting that they asked for. If the mentor had felt this way and placed his own value judgments on the mentee being late, he might not have engaged in guidance, advice, and feedback that helped Dr. Gaines achieve the levels of success he currently enjoys, and he also would have precluded a positive, deep relationship from developing. In my interview with this mentor, I asked him about this first meeting and how he approaches practicing patience with his mentees.

"I just think it's important to be extremely patient, at least at the very beginning, because you just never know the full story," he told me. "It's definitely easier to do that with younger kids, but we should practice that with adults too. Just because you're talking to an adult, you can't assume they've had a voice like yours in their lives before they met you. Maybe what you're saying is the first time they've ever had someone give them that feedback and that guidance, so I just don't think it's right to dismiss people immediately because they don't act the way you think they should. It can really get in the way of something beautiful, like what John has achieved in his life so far.

"To be clear, I'm not saying something like being late is acceptable. What he told you is right: time is the one thing we never get back. All I'm saying is to give people a couple of chances. Give them feedback, and then see what they do with it. Trust me—I'd love to spend more time with family and loved ones, and that can't happen if I'm spending time in meetings with new people who are showing up late. But I think what mentors should do is stay patient and accessible for a little bit longer. For me, if someone is late once, I'll tell them the same thing I told John. If they show up late a second time, I'll start thinking this might be a pattern. If this happens and they ask for another meeting, I'll schedule one with them but I won't go out of my way to move things around on my calendar to make it work and it'll kind of just be whenever there's an opening.

"If they're late a third time, that's when this relationship no longer becomes a priority. I'll still meet with them because I don't really want to turn people away if I can be of service to them, but maybe we won't get something on the calendar for weeks at a time, and when we do get something on the calendar, I might double-book them because there's a chance they don't show up or they're late anyway. I think this kind of approach is something mentors can consider. It's a balance between being fair to yourself by spending time on the relationships that the other people are investing in just as much as you are, while still remaining patient and accessible to people who can really benefit from your presence in their life and the value you might be able to provide them."

Inequities in accessibility to resources and mentors do exist, and it is our collective responsibility to reduce them. Creating meaningful relationships and genuine connections with others is hard enough as it is. Do your part as an intentional mentor to remain accessible, open, and patient with potential mentees for as long as possible.

AVAILABILITY

In addition to being readily accessible, you must also make sure your mentee knows that you are *available* as a resource to them. The distinction here is that accessibility means that you can be easily reached and your mentee doesn't have to go through too much trouble to connect with you. Availability, meanwhile, means that you are fully present during meetings and interactions with your mentee and that you are committed to making the most of the time you spend with them. This is a major second step in developing a relationship with your mentee. You must regularly invite your mentee to meet with you, consistently let them know that you are there for them, and be present and engaged during your meetings. While verbal invitations and reminders are helpful, your availability can be demonstrated with even more impact through your actions. Alvin Snow Jr. is an example of someone who benefited from his mentor taking steps to make himself available.

Alvin became Eastern Washington University's first basketball All-American in 2004. After graduating from college, he enjoyed a successful international basketball career for more than a decade. He is currently a sports agent and CEO of Worldwide Sports Management. He integrates this work into his personal mission of finding unique ways to support both kids and adults to push for greatness and elevate themselves and each other. Before all of his current success, Alvin met his mentor, Chad Smith.

"I met Chad when I was in middle school," Alvin told me. "He worked for the Central Area Youth Association in Seattle, and we had a lot of similar interests. He tutored me in math. Of course, a big thing we connected on was basketball. I just remember that he would pick me up before school and take me to the community center to get a workout in and get some shots up. Then he'd drive me back home so I could get ready for school. Now here's the crazy thing: Chad lived right next to the community center and I lived across town, like fifteen or twenty minutes away. That means Chad would wake up, drive over to my place, pick me up, and then drive all the way back with me to the community center that was right next to where he lived. Then, after our early morning workout, he'd drive me all the way back to my place so I could go to school, and he'd drive all the way back to where he lived.

"I was just a young kid, so I didn't really get how much he was doing. I had no idea how much gas costed or anything like that. I didn't even fully appreciate that, if I was waking up at 6:00 AM for him to pick me up, that meant he was waking up even earlier than that, just to come pick a kid up to go get some extra work in at the gym. Honestly, I think it took me five or six years, around the time I was a junior in high school, to finally have a full appreciation for all the work he was doing in order to make himself available. It's just wild. I really can't believe he did all that. But stuff like that, all the work, all the patience, all the things he did to be available, I think that's why we're still in touch and why we're still close."

Chad, now a successful financial advisor, told me that this is the type of work that goes into being a good mentor. "I've had the opportunity to be around successful people I respect because of my line of work, and something I've noticed about them is that they are able to handle a ton of work and responsibility without making it seem overwhelming," he said. "There are people I've been around who make me feel like I'm one of one. It's really unbelievable sometimes what they do for me. I know how much work it requires. Then I'll see them in different contexts and I realize that, while they make me feel like I'm one of one, they actually do the same thing for twenty-seven other people. They have their own families and kids that they're giving attention to. And it's just amazing how they're able to balance all that work and effort, make each of these people feel special and supported, and also make it seem so seamless and not at all overwhelming.

"I think that's what good mentors do. I think you need to make meaningful impacts on as many people as you can with whom the relationship clicks. That takes a lot of work, but it's just what you do. And you can't have a meaningful impact on others if you aren't consistently available to those people. Like Alvin said, he doesn't think he fully understood all the work that went into building the relationship because he was so young at the time. I think if you want to be a mentor to someone, you can't expect to see the fruits of your labor pay off and you can't expect your mentee to appreciate everything you do. That can't be why you do the things you do. You have to do what you can to help them and provide them with value without expecting anything in return. That takes patience, consistency, and commitment. Again, it's not easy, but it's just what good mentors do.

"I coached seventh and eighth graders in AAU basketball, and the thing that I was committed to was helping my players gain the knowledge they didn't know they needed. I was preparing them for what a two-hour practice would look like in high school and for the concepts that I knew they'd have to master in high school. I probably sacrificed some wins in the short term by focusing more on their long-term learning. That meant I'd be experiencing more of the losses with them, and other coaches who got them as they grew older would get more of the wins. Since I was teaching them concepts that they were still a couple of years away from truly being ready for, I was part of all the struggles that come with the learning curve, especially for kids and young adults.

"But by the time the head coach got them as freshmen, these kids were ready for high school basketball. By the time they got to the varsity team, the concepts and nuances were things they were introduced to in seventh grade and refined in eighth grade. I had several of those kids come back to me when they were juniors in high school and tell me, 'All those things we worked on when I was in eighth grade finally make sense to me now!' That's really one of the best moments for me as a mentor: the memories I have of the kids I provided mentorship for coming back four years later and say, 'I get it now. Thank you.'"

APPROACHABILITY

In addition to being easily reachable and fully present as much as possible, the final ability that you should establish is approachability. In many ways, this is related to being a "get to" type of mentor, as described in Chapter 1. It's important to be viewed by your mentee as someone they are comfortable spending time with, especially when a large part of your role as a mentor is to challenge them to be better. An important element to being approachable is to practice a high level of patience as your mentee goes through the growing pains of learning new things.

One mentor I interviewed told me that she has a multi-step approach when mentoring student workers at the university where she works. "I need to see my mentees implement the recommendations I give them and things I teach them," she said. "I also need to make sure I give enough opportunities for them to put what they learn into practice while still keeping a high level of expectation. For technical tasks at work, I break down my approach. First, I tell the person I'm mentoring what to do. The second step is for me to show them what I explained. It's really important to not just explain what to do verbally [or through written manuals and handbooks], but to also give people who are learning something new the opportunity to witness what this looks like in action. The third step is for the mentee to show that they know how to do what I taught them by themselves. I'll be there to observe and supervise, and they'll have the opportunity to ask me anything they need to as they're getting the hang of it.

"All through this three-step process, mentees can ask me questions or use me as a resource. I give some leeway—maybe two or three times—for them to ask me the same question before I start addressing what the disconnect is or what might be getting in the way of them fully understanding how to do certain things at work. I make it very clear to all my mentees early on that these are the steps and the time to ask questions is throughout this entire process. It's important to set their expectations up front and make sure we're on the same page about how we'll make sure they learn what they need to, as well as the timeline for them to be self-sufficient in executing on those tasks. It definitely takes a lot of patience and time, but that's the space you have to create as a mentor in order for your mentees to be able to truly learn what they need to."

In addition to remaining patient as mentees are putting new things they've learned into practice, it's important to practice a high level of grace from the outset of the relationship so that your mentee feels comfortable opening up to you and trusting you. One mentor-mentee pair I interviewed met each other through their church. When I asked the mentee what he appreciates most about his mentor (who provides him with personal-life mentorship), he told me that his mentor is extremely approachable. In my interview with the mentor, I asked him what goes into being approachable.

"I think that's the biggest piece to being a mentor, because a relationship can't be built if you don't provide a foundation," he said. "You can respond to emails, texts, and calls immediately. You can make time for a meeting. You can have the important experience and expertise for whatever a person might need. But none of that matters if you aren't approachable. I know plenty of people who check every box you'd want out of a mentor, but they just aren't approachable. They kind of intimidate you, and they wind up never passing along all this great knowledge and perspective they have, all because nobody feels comfortable talking to them.

"Being approachable starts with not being judgmental. I think that's important in two respects: asking questions without judgment, and then listening without judgment. When I'm trying to provide guidance and perspective, it's really important for me to create a space where it's possible for the other person to receive it. That can only happen if the person I'm mentoring feels like I'm encouraging their efforts more than I'm judging their shortcomings. The other thing to keep in mind is that being approachable is something for the long haul. No one is going to invite me to give my perspective about parenting or their relationship with their spouse without having a whole lot of trust built into our relationship. That level of trust is built over a long period of time. It takes a lot of commitment, patience, consistency, and persistence."

Change, learning, and growth take time. Failure will be a part of the process for your mentee as you provide them with guidance. Don't forget the emotions you might have felt and the times you lacked confidence when you were young, inexperienced, or new in a role. Mentors I interviewed told me that it takes anywhere from a year to a year-and-a-half to truly grasp the responsibilities of their job, so it's important for you as a mentor to be patient when providing guidance for new employees. Personal-life mentorship is even more abstract and therefore takes even longer for a mentee to grasp concepts, particularly when you are mentoring children and young adults.

Regardless of the type of mentorship you are providing, patience is paramount. As a mentor, it might be helpful to consider your role as a *warm demander*. This term, borrowed from the K-12 education field (particularly when incorporating concepts of equity in the classroom), describes teachers who hold their students to high standards but simultaneously provide them with the support and confidence to achieve their potential. I think the idea of a warm demander can be applied to good mentors. This concept does not need to be limited to mentors who provide guidance for young children; you can adopt it even if you are mentoring adults, personally or professionally. No matter what steps you take to be a warm demander, you will always need to practice patient persistence to help them achieve their potential.

I don't want to pretend that patience, particularly over a long period of time as a mentor, is always easy to practice. It's a fine balance between remaining patient enough for a mentee to grow while also accurately assessing whether your mentee is doing the work required to progress toward realizing their potential. On a personal level, I'll admit that I struggle with practicing patience in certain situations. I did, however, hear stories and anecdotes over the months of interviews I conducted that I'll keep in mind whenever I find it challenging to be patient. One of these stories came from Francis Williams, a mentor I was fortunate to interview.

As a state championship-winning high school basketball coach and one of the godfathers of AAU basketball in the state of Washington (the *New York Times*, ESPN the Magazine, and Sports Illustrated have recognized him as one of the people directly responsible for Seattle becoming a hotbed of high school basketball), Francis has also had an illustrious career on the business and media sides of the sport. He was a consultant to the Adidas grassroots basketball marketing unit, has worked with the radio broadcast and community relations team for the Seattle SuperSonics, was a scout for the Charlotte Hornets, and is currently a college basketball studio and in-game analyst for ROOT SPORTS. He has also worked with CBS Sports Television as a color analyst and sideline reporter, and has been an in-game analyst for ESPN, NBATV, and NBA.com.

The success that Francis has enjoyed in his career cannot be denied, and it makes sense that people would seek out his mentorship. However, as our interview progressed, I realized that Francis' value as a mentor goes far beyond his résumé. Much more important than his work experiences are his commitment to the relationships in his life, the steps he takes to validate his mentees, and his consistency in helping the people he mentors push toward a better future. A constant theme of his approach to these aspects was patience. Toward the end of our interview, I asked him why he thinks he's able to remain so persistent and patient with the people he mentors, particularly when so many people struggle to practice these behaviors.

"The absolute reason I'm patient comes back to a life story of mine," he explained. "I moved to Muskogee, Oklahoma, when I was seven years old. There was a couple, Mr. and Mrs. Jordan, who were our neighbors a couple of houses down from us. On top of being in their late seventies, Mr. Jordan was also blind. This is back when people still got their checks in the mail and went into town to pay the phone bill, the electric bill, the water bill, and all the other bills in person.

"Mr. Jordan would get his disability checks delivered on the first of every month. When I was eleven, my mom—because she thought I was responsible—told me it was my job to get Mr. Jordan on the first of every month and take him into town to handle his monthly affairs. Again, I'm eleven and he's blind. I'd have to get a cab, hold his arm, get on his side so I could guide him to the cab, help him write his checks, make sure he was getting proper change if he was getting cash . . . I did that with Mr. Jordan every single month for two or three years until he passed away.

"That experience taught me the value of patience at a very young age. That's been refined over time. Now at my age and with my life experiences, I've learned more about patience from a different perspective. I was diagnosed with cancer in September 2016. There were days I was going through chemotherapy when I just couldn't do things for myself, so others had to do them for me. Between that experience and what I learned from what I was responsible for with Mr. Jordan, I've always felt that, when I'm in a situation where someone can't do something for themselves, I need to be willing to help them if I can. That requires patience. I think my patience is a huge part of any success I've had in being a mentor, or even a mentee. That patience was built over fifty years ago."

I'm confident that what Francis shared with me will be at the front of my mind when I'm finding it difficult to remain patient. In the hours we spent talking, he added a new lens for me to consider as I try my best to improve an area in which I need to be better. His story serves as a nice example for the next piece of value that mentors can bring to the lives of those they provide guidance for: providing mentees with *perspective*.

CHAPTER 7

PERSPECTIVE

A number of mentors I interviewed for the research study that informed this book spoke on the importance of "busting myths" about mentorship. A necessary first step is often to deconstruct assumptions about what mentorship entails in order to truly provide value as a mentor. One of the biggest myths about being a mentor is that it is your job to provide solutions to your mentee. Mentees frequently come into these relationships with a challenge they are looking to navigate (these problems can be as abstract as feeling lost about their future) and expect their mentor to be solution-oriented. Solutions are certainly of value, but they are typically the goal of conversations between mentors and mentees in very narrow and technical contexts where a simple answer will suffice. The much bigger piece of value that mentors add is to provide *perspective*.

Rather than give a singular solution as part of your feedback, your true role as a mentor is to instead redefine and reframe the questions that your mentee comes to you with. As a result, you are expanding the ways in which your mentee is thinking about their challenges, opportunities, and life in general. By definition, expanding the set of considerations for your mentee actually makes what they are coming to you with more complex than they initially thought. This means that your mentee will quickly feel as though they are even further away from finding an answer than they thought. At first, many mentees will be resistant to this owing to the discomfort they will feel because you are not matching their expectations of simply providing a resolution (or steps toward one) to their challenges. Effectively communicating your points is key, as you risk losing the commitment and buy-in of your mentee.

Your role as a mentor is not about making life easier for your mentee. Any good mentor will readily admit that life is anything but easy. Rather, your responsibility is to help your mentee have a more realistic outlook on life itself. This entails tough conversations in which your mentee comes to you for answers, only for you to push them to rethink the questions they are asking. While you might not be providing your mentee with a simplification of what to consider as they make decisions and take actions, this approach will allow your mentee to learn that their final destination is less important than the journey itself. As one of the mentees I interviewed said, "I used to head into meetings with my mentor thinking I had a good idea of what needed to be done and that I just needed help figuring out how to do those things. For the first couple of months, I left every meeting with him feeling like I had more questions than when I went into the meeting. As frustrating as that sounds, it was actually amazing, and it made me look forward to the next meeting with him because he was changing my thought process. He was getting me to challenge assumptions I had about what the task was, which then changed my considerations of how to go about accomplishing my goals.

"It's transformative to go through that process, because I literally think about things differently now. Before, I would be so focused on the *what* and the *how* of what I needed to do, because I knew how much work it would take to figure those out. He got me to start thinking one step before that: *why* do I need to do what I think I need to do? Figuring out the right answer to that question is huge, because once I have that, it informs what I do and how I do it, and it almost makes it easier to figure those details out. It's a whole lot of work to figure out the *why*, but it makes way more sense to spend my time trying to figure out what the right question is rather than to spend my time working really hard just to answer the wrong question."

This fundamental shift in thinking provides mentees with opportunities to learn, grow, and develop past the scope of what they might come to you with. As a mentor, you should consider that you might be able to "expand the scope" of the value you provide your mentee. After all, mentees don't know what they don't know. In addition to helping your mentee with what they are asking, you should look to leverage your experiences and expertise to put things on their radar as areas of exploration for growth and development. Again, this shift in thinking is difficult for many mentees to come to terms with. Therefore, it is important for you to be as intentional as possible with your approach to providing perspective for your mentee. There are a handful of characteristics to display, steps to take, and considerations to keep in mind as you provide your mentee with perspective.

AUTHENTICITY AND VULNERABILITY

Along with the myth of a mentor's value lying in their ability to provide solutions and answers to their mentee's challenges, another false perception is that mentors need to be perfect. "While it's important for a mentor to be someone that mentees can look up to and respect [both in terms of what they have accomplished and how they live their lives], it is paramount that mentees do not idealize or idolize their mentors," Bob Zellner told me. "When you do that with your leaders and mentors, you risk falling into cultism. You risk the movement and the actions you're committed to faltering and losing momentum if you make it about a *leader* or a *mentor* rather than about the *cause* that you're driving forward. A couple of dangerous things can happen if you idealize and idolize your mentor. One is that they might be exposed; some people can pretend to be perfect, but they have other motivations that aren't apparent at the outset. Another thing that can happen, like in the case of Dr. Martin Luther King Jr., is that you might unfortunately lose the person. But your cause and your commitment to the right behaviors shouldn't disappear as a result. The guiding principles shouldn't disappear, but you risk that happening when you idealize and idolize mentors. Mentees shouldn't do that, and good mentors shouldn't let that happen."

In an effort to guard against the risk of being idealized and idolized, two behaviors you can practice are *authenticity* and *vulnerability*. These behaviors will also help your mentee trust you, which will allow you to provide value by giving them perspective instead of straightforward solutions to their questions. Authenticity requires you to have open and honest conversations, both in terms of having confidence in areas where you are strong, as well as acknowledging areas where you have opportunities for growth and improvement. If you don't know the answer to a question posed by your mentee, or if topics you discuss are not in your area of expertise, don't be hesitant to say so early in the conversation. While you (as well as your mentee) may initially think that mentors should have all the answers and be infallible in order to be good mentors, there is actually much more value added to the relationship if you are fully transparent and genuine. This comes back to being a "get to" type of mentor; after all, how can anyone think you are a "get to" person if you aren't being your authentic self?

According to Dr. Brené Brown, author of *Daring Greatly*, vulnerability is the source of authenticity. Dr. Brown's breakthrough research on the power of vulnerability has been well documented in her best-selling books and TED Talks. It's no surprise that both mentees and mentors in my study cited the importance of mentors practicing vulnerability. "Being vulnerable doesn't mean you're weak; it means you're a person," said one of the mentees I interviewed. "Trust is such a huge part of mentorship, and I need to feel like I know my mentor as a person. I don't want someone robotic as a mentor, and I certainly don't want someone who acts as though they're perfect. More precisely, I don't want a mentor who's unwilling to share their imperfections in the sense of challenges, difficulties, or even failures they've experienced. I used to think the best mentors were the perfect ones.

"I used to think to myself, *Why would I want to learn from someone who makes just as many mistakes as I make, if not more?* I always thought I needed to be learning from the best. That's what I thought when I was younger. But I realized two pretty important things as I've grown up and refined what I think successful mentorship and a good mentor look like. First, I realized nobody is perfect. Anyone pretending to be perfect isn't being honest and authentic. At a certain point, it just can't last, and as a mentee, it's dangerous to put yourself in a position to wake up one day and realize this person you thought was perfect actually isn't perfect, and they did nothing to stop you from thinking that they were.

"Second, as much as I thought I wanted to be around perfection so that I could learn from it, I realized what a hit to my confidence it was to constantly feel like I would never be able to be as good as them, no matter how hard I tried. It's definitely important to look up to your mentor, but there needs to be some level of balance. I just think you're chasing madness if you're following someone thinking that their life is problem-free and that maybe one day your life is going to be problem-free, just like theirs. It's more about their ability and capacity to handle the problems, challenges, and stressors in their lives. It's about accepting that those things will always be there, even for the people you think are amazing. It's about realizing that you think they are amazing because they've found ways to address those things. I think the best mentors are the ones who are willing to spend the time explaining how they make sense of the tough times they've experienced and try to add value in your life. It's just so important for mentors to be open, honest, vulnerable, and emotionally intelligent when they're with their mentees."

A mentor I interviewed offered his perspective on the importance of vulnerability when he provides mentorship, including an anecdote on why he finds practicing that behavior to be so powerful and impactful. "I think it's really important for mentors to level the playing field by expressing their shortcomings and challenges to mentees they have developed close relationships with," he said. "My wife and I used to lead a parenting class for our church and community. As someone with a special-needs son, I thought I had a perspective that might be useful and could add a unique lens to what most people think of when they think about parenting classes. My wife and I were sought after as facilitators for the class, and I think a big reason is because I was committed to sharing anecdotes and personal stories with the class about my experience as a father.

"As hard as it was, I shared stories of times when the windows in my house were open and my neighbors would hear me speaking sternly to my children, scolding them, and at times raising my voice. Even the best, most patient parents lose their tempers. It's hard to talk about because I'm obviously embarrassed by those instances and those stories, but they're important to share with people who are taking steps to be more proactive and intentional about their parenting styles. It's important to let them know that no matter how hard they try, they *will* have moments of frustration and embarrassment. They'll have moments that they'll look back on and feel just terrible about themselves and how they acted toward their kids. I'm open, honest, and vulnerable with these stories I share. I freely admit my embarrassment about it, but I also make it clear that I've been able to learn from those times.

"The participants in the class are sitting there thinking they came to listen to an 'expert,' but wind up realizing that the 'expert' actually started where they are as parents. They start thinking they're the same as you. They connect with you; they trust you. They appreciate your authenticity and your vulnerability, and they're even more open to the idea that they can learn from you. All of that comes back to the fact that you're able to show that you're the same as them. You started where they currently are and you've grown, and because you've shown growth in your process, it gives them hope for their own future. It also gives them the confidence that you can be of value through the perspective you can give as they start practicing the skills needed for their future."

THE POWER OF WHY

Earlier in the chapter, I shared a quote from a mentee explaining the importance of reflecting on *why* they were taking certain actions before moving to the *what* and the *how*. Researcher Simon Sinek delivered an influential TED Talk about the power of *why*. He explained that a common theme between successful organizations (such as Apple) and successful people (such as the Wright brothers and Dr. Martin Luther King Jr.) is the ability to invert the typical process of decision making and communication. While most people and organizations start with *what* they do before moving to *how* and then *why* they do what they do (many don't even reach this last step), Sinek said the successful ones start with the *why* before filtering down to *how* they do *what* they do. Inspiring your mentee to practice this approach is integral to fulfilling your role as their mentor.

Mentors and mentees—in both professional and personal-life relationships—agreed on the importance of mentees needing to understand the logic, rationale, and "why" behind the advice and feedback their mentors provide. Whether it was mentorship in K-12 education, higher education administration, the technology sector, military, nonprofits, or personal-life contexts, "the power of why" consistently came up during the interviews. "As a mentor, if you suggest to your mentee that they should do something, they can usually do it on their own," one mentor told me. "But if you don't connect the dots on *why* they're doing it, or at the very least hold a discussion in which they can ask you about the rationale and logic behind your recommendations, the probability that they're going to *incorrectly* reproduce the steps you suggested is much higher."

Another mentor explained it this way: "My goal with my mentees is to make sure they're not successful just when I'm around, but that they can choose the right paths and do the right things even when I'm not there. That's what true learning is. Some mentees don't come looking for you; they don't even know they can benefit from mentorship. It doesn't help to just tell them what to do. They're smart enough to follow directions, but they aren't really learning anything. I need to make sure they can think for themselves, because I'm not around all the time, and these are kids who face tough situations every single day. I'm doing them a disservice by only explaining what to do or how to do it. I need them to connect to the reasoning behind it all.

"There are other mentees I have who are super driven and seek me out to ask for my guidance. They'll run through a wall to make sure they do what I recommend. That's not the learning opportunity though. Where they can benefit the most is the same as the first group of mentees who don't seek me out: understanding the *why*. If they understand the core of what my suggestions are based on, they can make their own sense of it. There'll inevitably be a time when they're faced with a decision in the moment and I'm not there to help them. I need to make sure they're able to figure things out on their own in those situations. If I simply tell them what to do and how to do it, *I* become the solution to the challenges they're facing. If I'm not there, that means their ability to solve their challenge is gone, too. That doesn't happen if I give my perspective and the reasons behind that perspective."

Sometimes, providing the *why* doesn't even have to come from a direct conversation in which you explain the rationale and logic behind the advice you give. In some situations, a mentee will come to you because they are having difficulties with another person or group of people, and you can use your experience and perspective to explain where they may be coming from and why. "My mentor provides me with perspective about personal life questions and things I'm thinking about," one mentee told me. "She's a great person to go to for a lot of things. One topic that stands out is my relationship with my family and my parents. As with any family, there are times when communication with my parents could be improved. Sometimes that gets really frustrating. My mentor is the perfect voice to lend some perspective in those times and a big reason why is because she's a mother. She's able to give me a parent's perspective of the situation. Through that, I'm able to see where my parents are coming from and why they're approaching things the way they are. It opens my eyes to things that I'm not seeing. She's able to use her experiences as a mom to get the message to land with me, or at least get me to understand why my parents are approaching things the way they are. Having her perspective helps me understand the reasons and logic behind the interactions and communication with my parents in certain situations, and that really helps a lot."

The goal of this chapter is to impress upon you the reasons you should focus on providing perspective rather than simple solutions to your mentee. Your approach to providing perspective is much more complex than giving recommendations, suggestions, and considerations to expand your mentee's thinking; you need to explain *why* these are your suggestions. While the process of implementing your suggestions will require time and effort from your mentee, the real value in their relationship with you comes from building their capacity to understand the logic behind the approaches you suggest. This way, your mentee can not only learn how to apply logical frameworks to their problem solving on their own (explained in Chapter 8) but they can also decide whether your approach and thoughts align with their own personal core values. Always keep in mind that, as a mentor, it is your job to keep the mentorship relationship *mentee-focused*—you are responsible for idea generation and facilitating your mentee learning more about themselves. You can achieve these goals by remaining committed to explaining the *why* behind your suggestions.

BUILDING (AUTHENTIC) CONFIDENCE

Arguably the biggest piece of perspective you can provide for your mentee is that they are not only someone who has a tremendous amount of value currently, but they also have the potential for a bright future. We all have our insecurities, and this self-doubt is heightened in periods when we are navigating uncertain times. In these contexts, your support and encouragement can be invaluable for a mentee. Giving your mentee an asset-based framing of themselves (as opposed to a deficit-based framing) can be crucial for their development, particularly if you are one of the few voices in their lives reminding them of their strengths. Oftentimes, a significant area of opportunity for a mentee's growth and development is simply having more confidence. However, building confidence in your mentee is a more nuanced process than simply encouraging them. Chad Smith, a mentor I mentioned in Chapter 6, had a clear explanation on why building confidence in a mentee isn't as straightforward as you might think.

"A key piece of providing mentorship is to give your mentee encouragement, but you need to be very careful about not just being a cheerleader who gives positive feedback on everything they're doing or thinking of doing," Chad said. "In fact, blindly supporting them on everything can be counterproductive. They might try to go after a goal simply because you encouraged them to, even if deep down you knew it likely wouldn't work out. I completely understand not wanting to kill someone's dream or shutting them down, particularly a young person. But you have to balance that with a commitment to providing them with an understanding of reality.

"Sometimes, your words of support can mean the world to them, and if they fail, they'll feel like they failed you. It winds up being even worse than if you had just been honest with them. Building confidence in a mentee is important, but I think what mentors need to focus on is building *authentic confidence*."

From the interviews I conducted, I found four ways to build authentic confidence in your mentee. You should use a combination of all four approaches (depending on the situation) rather than only applying one or two.

One mentor I interviewed transferred skills that are useful in her professional work over to the personal-life mentorship she provides for her friends and community members. "My role as a Bereavement Coordinator for a local hospice company gives me the opportunity to support grieving families," she told me. "One thing I do in my role is I *normalize their feelings* and let them know that it is okay to feel how they do. It's such a powerful thing for people to realize they have permission to feel the way they do. It's the jumping-off point for them to realize for themselves that these feelings are part of the process of healing, and it helps build their inner confidence that they'll be able to heal. I use that same approach of normalizing feelings when it comes to mentoring the college students who come to my home for weekly dinners. I let them know that it's okay to be themselves and to feel how they do. I think that's the first step in being able to build your self-confidence."

The second approach to building authentic confidence is a slight extension of normalizing the feelings of your mentee: in addition to giving them permission to be themselves and feel how they feel, you can let them know that *they are not alone* in what they are experiencing. This is a great approach if you have concrete examples of how others (yourself included, perhaps) have shared the same feelings of self-doubt in the experiences they are going through.

I interviewed a mentor-mentee pair of attorneys. "I met my mentor in my first job out of law school, and I really learned a lot from her," the mentee said. "One of the biggest things she gave me was perspective. At the time, I thought all that mattered was whether or not I won my cases that went to trial. It's hard to get your footing in your first job out of law school. It really takes a lot of time to get the hang of things, and my confidence was definitely affected by it. Even as I was picking up skills that helped make me a better attorney, I was still really stressed about having cases that I just didn't feel like I could win. The way my mentor approached the conversation when I told her I was feeling like this really helped build my confidence."

"I told him that this is something every other attorney at our office has gone through," the mentor told me. "Literally every single person at our work gets cases like this when they start. Hell, I still had those kinds of cases at the time, and I had years of experience! That's just what some cases are: they aren't winnable because of a lack of evidence or whatever it may be. The first thing I had to get him to realize is that absolutely nobody at work was going to think less of him for not winning those cases. I needed him to realize that, not only would everyone completely understand if he didn't win, but also that nobody was expecting him to win those cases because of the nature of the case, the available evidence—all of that makes it pretty much an unwinnable case.

"Now, that isn't an excuse to not go out there and give it your best shot. He fully understood how he could use it as a learning experience in how to prepare for trial, how to cross-examine witnesses, how to build the best case he possibly could, etc. But it was important for him to get some perspective and realize the truth: this isn't unique to him and by no means should he let this affect his confidence level about his ability to be a good lawyer."

Another way to build authentic confidence in your mentee is to point to specific qualities they possess or actions they have demonstrated in the past to let them know that *they are built for success*. This is probably the most common version of improving the self-confidence of your mentee, but focus on connecting the dots for them on how specific examples of behaviors they are practicing (or have practiced) will seamlessly set a strong foundation for future success in the challenge they are navigating.

I spoke to an individual who provides mentorship for high school students. "Some of the high school students I mentor are going to be first-generation college students, and there's a lot of nervousness around that for them," she told me. "There's stress around the fact that their peers who aren't first generation are set up for success and will have help that they don't have access to. There's this sense of imposter syndrome and this fear that they're going to be exposed once they get to college. I make it clear to them that they're not alone in feeling this way, and I even make sure they know that students who aren't first generation have similar feelings of insecurity around their ability to succeed after high school.

"But I also remind them of what they've accomplished so far. I point to all the work they've done in high school and all the success they've already achieved. I remind them that they navigated the college application process themselves. I cite specific behaviors they've demonstrated that they can apply in college as well, including the fact that they reached out to me and are having these conversations. I try to give them perspective that not everyone is proactive enough to seek out and ask for mentorship, but they did that! I even go into some really small details, like how they wrote a great email to me to set up some time for us to talk, or how something as simple as taking notes during our meeting—which they thought to do themselves—is a signal that they already understand a lot about the right behaviors that will contribute to their success.

"As they start to realize they're doing all these little things without even having to think about them, and they all kind of snowball into what it takes to succeed in college, they start to gain that self-confidence and shed some of those fears and insecurities. They start to realize that they've earned their seat at the table, and that all the things that went into getting that seat is at the foundation of what's going to lead them to future success."

The fourth and final way to drive authentic confidence in your mentee is by *leveraging your perspective as a mentor to provide your mentee with external validation.* Given that Chad Smith kicked off this section with his explanation of authentic confidence, it seems only fitting that he be the one to provide insights for this final approach of increasing a mentee's self-confidence. "Before I became a financial advisor, I was a basketball coach. I was heavily involved in the AAU basketball scene and coached against Jason Terry [a nineteen-year pro in the NBA] from when he was twelve years old until he went to college. I knew Jason and his mom well. Back then, the AAU world was smaller. Even though we were all rivals, you played against each other so many times that the players and coaches from different teams all got really close. We were like a band of brothers.

"I saw his skill set firsthand, and I saw what was required for a guy like Jason to go from high school basketball in Seattle to the University of Arizona and win an NCAA Championship. I saw what Jason was doing against our team at a young age and how that translated to him being named conference player of the year as a senior in college and then be a lottery pick in the NBA Draft. I saw how for years when our team would play against Jason, I threw everything I could at him, and despite that, he would always make the right play and was always under control. I saw everything he was doing from a young age and how that translated to the next levels he played at. This means that when I stepped into a gym and was coaching younger kids after Jason was getting recruited by colleges, playing well at the college level, and then made it to the NBA, I could tell those kids, *I know what it takes; I've seen it before in someone I've coached against a ton of times, and you have what it takes to achieve that kind of success because I see you doing the same kinds of things right now.*

"To be clear, I didn't say that to every kid. But there were some kids that I'd come across who were just special. Again, young people, inexperienced people, mentees, whatever you want to call them—they're limited by the same thing: They don't know what they don't know. But given my set of experiences, what I had been around and what I had seen, I could give them some insight and perspective into that. I could let them know that I've seen this before in someone else, and I see it in you too. The ability to do that requires a mentor to be great at what they do and to have had their own experiences with success to be able to have that perspective. But if you're able to acquire that perspective as a mentor, it's your job to share it with the mentees it applies to. When you do that, you can really sense and see a shift in the level of confidence those mentees bring in their approach to the future."

OFFER OPTIONS

The early part of this chapter offered insight from a mentee who said that, for the first few months of conversation with his mentor, he would leave meetings with more questions than he had come in with. The driving force behind this phenomenon is that, when the mentor provided perspective, the mentor, by definition, was also expanding the menu of available *options* for his mentee to pursue moving forward. Perspective and options go hand in hand; as you provide perspective for your mentee, you can help them think critically about the options you bring to their attention as potential avenues to learn more about.

Francis Williams, a mentor I introduced in the previous chapter, gave me insights on what he considers when thinking of how best to frame the options that are available to his mentees. "I think the first part of what I'm going to say is what most people think of when they think of mentors providing options for their mentees. When I was a basketball coach, I knew that most players aspire to play at the highest levels. That's a great dream, but you're really up against it if you're thinking so narrowly about what makes sense for your next steps. One thing I always used to tell all the players, repeatedly, was that 0.2 percent of college athletes go on to play professional sports. That's just the data and those are the facts; you can't argue with that. For a lot of these kids, I had to reframe this outlook. I spent my time trying to explain that there's nothing wrong with thinking about mid-major conferences, Division II schools, Division III colleges, NAIA programs, or some junior colleges. First of all, those are just the levels at which they were getting recruited. Second, it's all about the right fit. It makes no sense to look down at these options as though they're below you and below your goals. There's no such thing as something like that being underneath you or not good enough for you if it really is what's right for you. That's the way you have respect for the game. I always told players, 'It's great that you have love for the game. But don't ever think there's something about the game that's below you, because that's *disrespecting* the game. You can love the game, but make sure you never disrespect the game.'

"Now, for the second part of what I'm going to say—this is the part that a lot of mentors don't think of when they think through providing options for the individuals they're mentoring. Before I was a basketball coach, I worked for the Security Department for Seattle Public Schools. I was friendly with the kids, and I'd always check in with them and see how they're doing. There was this one young woman who was absolutely brilliant. She was the valedictorian of her graduating class. I asked her about her plans after high school. I asked her where she was thinking of going to college after graduation. She told me she was thinking of the local community college.

"To be clear, there's nothing at all wrong with that plan. There's nothing wrong with going the community college route whatsoever. But again, she was the valedictorian of her entire class. This young woman, she could not only get into a lot of colleges around the country but she could go there for free. I'm not talking about financial aid like loans that she'd have to pay back; I'm talking about not paying a penny for college! So many colleges would love to have a young woman like this on their campus! She just wasn't aware that this was an option for her. It was clear right off the bat that that was her plan because she didn't have a voice in her life providing her with the guidance, or even the perspective, of the options and alternatives that were available to her. So, I connected her with a couple of the new school counselors at the high school who I knew well. I told them what I knew about how talented and smart she was. It was a team effort, and the school counselors made sure to let this young woman know that she had other options outside of the route that people immediately around her might have been taking, and that she could explore those options because the work she had done up until that point had earned her that right. She wound up going to the University of Washington after high school was over.

"I think these two stories capture the range of ways in which mentors can offer options to their mentees. For some people you mentor, you're going to have to reframe and refine their outlook on things. You're going to have to get them to understand that, mentally, they might be closing themselves off from options that are actually good for them. You need to change that outlook and mindset by reframing how they're looking at those options. On the other hand, you'll have some people you mentor who you need to encourage to think bigger. Whether it's because of a lack of confidence or a lack of knowledge, it doesn't matter; they're just not aware of options that they're qualified for. Offer them those options, and give them that perspective."

Providing perspective rather than solutions to your mentee is a key shift in thinking for your approach to mentorship. However, your perspective will only go so far in helping a mentee find the answers to the challenges and tough decisions they face. Therefore, as a mentor, you must continue to exert a positive influence on your mentee by facilitating their development of skills related to *problem solving*.

CHAPTER 8
PROBLEM SOLVING

*P*atience and persistence are the foundation of being a good a mentor. And providing your mentee with perspective rather than solutions should be a focal point of your approach to the role. However, none of these behaviors are enough when it comes to assisting your mentee with actually taking the actions to improve their effectiveness. It would be unfair for you as a mentor to expand the range of your mentee's thinking and not follow through as they navigate the considerations and the complexities you have added to their planning. The final step to being a good mentor is to support your mentee in the *problem-solving process.*

Think about it this way: the perspective you provide will tell your mentee *what* they need to consider about their current situation, while assistance in improving their problem-solving skills will inform *how* they go about improving their future (and be sure to explain the *why* in both cases!). If you don't know the answer to one of your mentee's questions, or you don't think you have the proper experience to help them with a specific area of advice they need, don't simply say that you can't help them. Remember, your role as a mentor is to provide perspective, not solutions, and to help your mentee learn a general problem-solving approach that will work for them. One way you can do this is to connect your mentee to someone who might be of more help in that specific area. If you don't have someone in your immediate network who can help them, be a thought partner and brainstorm with your mentee on how to go about finding resources that may be of help to them.

I was once told that "I don't know" is never an acceptable response; however, "I don't know, but . . ." is perfectly valid. Not knowing an answer is acceptable and understandable, but as you grow and gain more experience, you must have a process and structure in place for creative problem solving. Inexperienced and new mentees may not have that capacity yet, but as a mentor, you need to be able to model this behavior for them and be seen as someone who is invested in helping them learn their own problem-solving techniques. Earlier in the book, I mentioned a mentee who is a Product Manager at Google. As she told me during our interview, "I really appreciated how my mentor took the time to explain her thought process and overall approach to problem solving for making decisions as a Product Manager. Since I switched roles from being a Designer to being a Product Manager, it was important for me to hear that perspective. The bigger thing, though, was that she helped me develop my own problem-solving skills. The decisions I have to make in this role not only change from project to project but also take on different forms *within* projects themselves. But that doesn't mean that you can't have a framework or a general system of problem solving to help inform those decisions.

"One of the biggest things I can say is how important it is for mentors to make the problem-solving process feel collaborative. There's a really fine balance that mentors need to strike. On the one hand, you need to give your mentee the space and the autonomy to have ownership over their work and ultimately be responsible for the decisions they make. Hopefully that winds up being a good outcome, which means they'll feel responsible for the success they've achieved. That being said, I think it's important for mentors to also make mentees feel like this is *our* thing to figure out, rather than the mentee simply using the mentor as a resource to get to their goal. The most fulfilling mentorship relationships that I've been a part of are the ones where it feels collaborative, we figure it out together, and it's not just a one-way street. I think that's what mentors should aim to provide for their mentees."

It's hard work to figure out how to strike that balance between giving your mentee enough autonomy to own their decisions, actions, and chosen path while still making them feel like you are there as a thought partner and collaborator in their journey. This chapter will outline three distinct ways to strike that balance. Don't simply focus on developing your capacity as a mentor in only one of these areas. True mentorship requires you to be able to deliver value to your mentee in a multitude of ways, and your mentee stands to benefit the most if you take all three of these pieces into account as you help them develop their problem-solving skills.

SYSTEMS (OF) THINKING

In the previous chapter, I laid out the case for you to focus on providing your mentee with perspective to expand their worldview and ways of considering their questions. An extension of providing perspective is helping your mentee build the capacity for *systems thinking* as they refine their approach to problem solving. Systems thinking is a way of helping your mentee view their questions and challenges through a lens that sees overall patterns, cycles, and structures that exist in systems, rather than specific, singular events that occur in a vacuum. This approach to problem solving is particularly useful in addressing complex problems, which are typically those in which you can provide your mentee with the most value. As a mentor, you can help your mentee see the different parts of what is going on around them as well as how these parts interrelate and influence each other. This provides a more nuanced and realistic (albeit complicated) map of the landscape for your mentee.

There are specific techniques you can use to help your mentee engage in systems thinking. For example, one mentor told me that she uses temporal jumps to help her mentees when they seem stuck in a narrow way of thinking and she needs to get them to think more broadly. "I'll ask them to envision the future," she said. "Depending on the context in which they're coming to me and the type of questions they have, that can be short term [in the span of the next few months] or it can be a few years into the future. Helping them get out of the current situation and start thinking about a specific time frame in the future is something that I've found works. I try to use visualization techniques by asking them questions like, 'In that period of time in the future, what is your ideal case scenario?' or 'What would you change in the future?' These kinds of questions can help get them talking and spur on generation of new ideas, but the biggest thing it does is it gets them to start thinking about new variables and new considerations, all on their own. As they start to name those things, I can add things I know they'll be likely to face as well. But it gives them some level of having to come up with the foundation of it themselves while also making it feel like we're doing this as a partnership.

"I want to make it clear that temporal jumps don't just need to be about the future. Sometimes, I've found it useful to ask my mentees to reflect back on things. I can ask them about what they would have changed, or about something they know now that they wish they had known in the past. Those types of questions and a backward jump help to get at the same type of considerations a forward temporal jump does, but mentees can leverage the benefit of hindsight. Again, it's all about getting them unstuck and out of a narrow line of thinking, which is a trap a lot of people fall into. You can't lose sight of how interconnected different pieces of a system are and how much more likely you are to make a good decision if you think about things in terms of a system. You don't need to have a full understanding of each piece of the system and how it works. I actually don't think anyone truly has a complete understanding of all systems and how they function at all times. But simply having awareness and not thinking of things in a vacuum is a huge step in the right direction, not just for mentees but for anyone who's making a decision."

In addition to systems thinking, you can help your mentee practice systems *of* thinking. The distinction here is that building systems of thinking gives your mentee frameworks for how to approach decisions. While volatility, uncertainty, complexity, and ambiguity are reasons why no two situations are the same (and therefore require different considerations to reach the optimal decision), it is important to make sure your mentee knows that there are some general, standardized methods they can use to create a structure for decision making.

One mentor gave me a great example of how he helps his mentees develop systems of thinking. "One of the things I tell people I'm able to help is that I think it all boils down to a thought process," he said. "You're going to have millions of decisions that you're going to have to make in your life. There are going to be benefits and there are going to be consequences that come out of the choice you make. I tell people for whom I've provided mentorship that, over time, we're going to work together to narrow down their thought process in a way that they're going to understand both the benefits and consequences of their choices.

"A lot of the people that I do what I can for in terms of support and guidance are young people in the community around me. There are a lot of opportunities for bad decisions to be made around here. There are some very serious things that young people in different parts of the community can get caught up in—gangs, drugs—you name it. Some of the home life and family situations of these kids are challenging, too. There are just a lot of choices young people in this area have to make between good and bad activities. There are a lot of times when they may be asked to go do something, and it comes down to whether or not they can stay away from a dangerous or risky situation. There are just a lot of things around here that kids can be tempted by. They know these things are wrong, but the opportunity still exists for them to get caught up in these types of things.

"I can't be there at all times to keep them out of trouble or make the right decision on their behalf. So, I try to give them a process of how to think about these things. If you're asked to do something and you have to think about whether or not you should do it because it might be a bad activity to be caught up in, then you probably shouldn't be doing it because it's a bad decision. If someone comes up to you and asks you to rob a bank with them, and they lay out all the money you can make from doing it, and you're going back and forth about whether you should go rob a bank with that person, that's a signal that you should probably not do that. If for some reason they get past that point and they're still considering the decision and leaning toward doing it, then I tell them, 'You should think to yourself, *If an adult who loves me and cares about me and is responsible for me were standing here right now, would they be okay with this?* If the answer is no, then you probably shouldn't be doing it.'

"'But if again you somehow get past that and you're still leaning toward doing that thing you shouldn't be doing, then you need to pick up your phone and call that adult. You should call me. Then I can tell you, or that other adult who has your best interests in mind can tell you, to stay away. If it's not that bad of an idea, you shouldn't have a problem calling an adult that's responsible for you in some way and telling them what you're about to do. It's about building a thought process and a system of finding a way to keep yourself out of trouble.'"

Helping your mentee with both systems thinking and systems *of* thinking will develop their problem-solving skills and help them engage in the proper decision making required for success. Make the process of improving your mentee's capacity for systems thinking a collaborative one by staying involved enough to have them feel like you are a teammate they can count on while also feeling empowered to make decisions autonomously. Let them know that you have the confidence in them to make the right decision as long as they are deliberate in engaging in systems thinking and having a system of thinking for the challenges they face.

WALK THE TALK

It's important to supplement the recommendations on how to incorporate systems thinking (and systems of thinking) into your mentee's problem-solving process by demonstrating these mindsets through your own actions. In other words, you have to be willing to *walk the talk*. This piece of the mentorship you provide is aligned with the discussions throughout this book about mentees paying close attention to opportunities to observe and experience a mentor in action and evaluate whether or not the potential mentor is the right fit for them. It will be harder for your mentee to buy in or fully understand what you try to facilitate with them if you are not living these approaches yourself. You must keep in mind that there are many ways in which your mentee can learn and accept guidance from you. While creating the space for the discussions plays a large role in your ability to be an effective mentor, don't forget to pay close attention to aligning your own actions with the recommendations and feedback you are providing.

One of the youngest interviewees in my research study, an undergraduate student, spoke to the importance of her mentor walking the talk. "I met my mentor when I was in seventh grade, but it turned into a true mentorship relationship when I was in high school," she told me. "Even in high school, I realized that the biggest reason I respected her and why I trusted her to be a mentor is that she led out of action, not just out of words. There was [and still is] such a perfect alignment between what she thinks, what she says, and what she does. I knew her in a variety of contexts, and one of them was that she was my basketball coach in high school. She had a very clear mission statement: to make women great off the court. She wanted us to be great people even outside of basketball. Everything she did drove that mission. She laid out ways for us to be great, both on and off the court. She explained why she was recommending the things that she was. From all of that, I was able to get a better sense of not just what to think, but *how* to think through things."

Established professionals echoed this sentiment as well. Another mentee I mentioned earlier, who is a consultant at Boston Consulting Group, described the value of seeing his mentor act in accordance with his recommendations. "My mentor is from my previous job before I started at BCG, when I worked at Booz Allen Hamilton as a Technology Consultant," he said. "That was my second job after I graduated from college. In my first job, I had a solid foundation of how to be a good consultant. I wanted to use my time at Booz Allen Hamilton to become even better. My mentor was on a couple of projects that I was on, and he'd give me some pointers.

"One of the main things he told me was that, even though the contract with a client might specify ten things we are responsible for, we should never be stopping at just that. We can always try to add more value. We can offer services that make sense to add to our existing contract. This way, we're expanding the scope of work, building a deeper relationship with our client by providing them with more value, and bringing in more value to Booz Allen Hamilton by rewriting the contract to expand the scope of work and increase the total worth of the contract. On a personal level, this is exactly what the development of a consultant should look like in order to land the next promotion: facilitating bringing in new work and new [or adjusted] contracts and business from clients.

"It always made sense to me when he'd tell me this after a client call or when we'd go out to lunch. But what really helped the most was literally being able to see and hear him pitch his 'extra' ideas to the client. I was able to pick up on how he connected the dots between the work we were already doing and the expansion of services he was offering. I was also able to observe how he pitched that idea, as well as the timeline of planting the seed with the client, all the way through to getting them to commit to a revised scope of work. It helped me expand my thinking and change how I thought about things. He made himself available for calls and answered all my questions when I needed more insight into *how* he thought through these things. All of that together has helped me improve my thought processes, ways of thinking, and approach to consulting and providing value to my clients."

Another way you might want to act in accordance with your thought processes is to "be in the trenches" with your mentee when the chance permits. "I work in University Housing, and there are times when we have to come in on Saturdays at 7:00 AM to move out furniture and get housing units ready," another interviewee told me. "My mentor works in the Housing Department as well but is a number of levels above me. None of the managers in the levels between my level and her level would show up for what they probably think is 'grunt work' to be done by the employees at the lowest levels of the department. I think that they think it's not their jobs to do that kind of work. But my mentor was there every single time, despite the fact that she was basically at as high a level as you can be. Not only that, but she would be the first one there, showing up thirty minutes early every time we had to do one of these cleanouts.

"The fact that she led by example was really powerful and helped build trust in the relationship. It wasn't just that she was in the work with all of us that was really inspirational; it was also that I was able to see her in action and how she thought through what needed to be done. She was so efficient and was always thinking three steps ahead. Being able to witness that has added to how I think about problem solving in my work. It wasn't just the Saturdays when I got to witness this. It was also during work discussions in the office, when a complaint came in from a student in one of our dorms and we had to figure out how to resolve the issue . . . Any of those times, I was able to see how she thought through problems and how to fix them. I saw the standard she held for herself and her office, and it made me think about the standard I should hold my work to. It made me realize that, if that was my standard for my work, I'd need to take a similar approach to problem solving as she did. I was able to see her thought process in action and that was really valuable for me to observe."

OFFER OPPORTUNITIES

In the previous chapter about providing perspective, I recommended you make sure to offer options as a way to expand your mentee's way of thinking. When it comes to supporting your mentee in the development of their problem-solving process and techniques, you should focus on *offering opportunities* to your mentee to showcase their decision-making approach. Being able to "walk the talk" isn't just about ensuring that your personal behaviors align with your espoused values when your mentee sees you in action; you also need to make sure to reinforce that what you are saying to your mentee about the value you see in them is not just lip service. By "inviting them to have a seat at the table" and giving them an opportunity (that they've earned) to practice leadership and take on an active role, you are allowing your mentee to get the necessary reps to develop and refine their methods, as well as building their confidence.

"My mentor brought me into a pretty major international assignment early in my Navy career," the former Admiral I mentioned earlier told me. "I was really amazed that he'd even think to bring me into that work because I was pretty young at the time and just getting started in my career. It definitely wasn't a normal assignment for someone at that stage in their career, but he vouched for me, and his voice carried some weight, given that he was eight or nine years ahead of where I was in my career. He was always really nice to me and built up my confidence by telling me that I was smart, a hard worker, and other things that go into finding success in any career. But the fact that he thought of me for this assignment really helped drive home those things he told me. I never really doubted that he meant what he was saying about my potential, but it's pretty much impossible to doubt it when someone gives you opportunities to work on things and contribute to projects that have a higher level of visibility and are good for your career.

"I think my mentor doing that really helped to build trust in a number of ways," he continued. "For one, I knew I could trust him to look out for me and keep me in mind for things that might help my career. Second, I could trust what he was telling me and that he really did believe in my potential and the success that I could have in my career. The vote of confidence he gave for me to be on this assignment was also a signal of the trust he had in me, because any work I did would be a reflection on him. If I didn't do something correctly, he'd have to be the one who answered to that. That also motivated me to work hard and make sure that I paid back the relationship that he was investing in with me."

Alicia Marini Bloom is another mentee I interviewed for my research. Currently the Staff Vice President of Business Development and Partnerships at a healthcare company, Alicia walked me through her career progression during our interview, and described the role her mentor played in her professional development. "I graduated from the University of Pennsylvania with a Master of Social Work degree and was looking for a job because my clinical rotation was wrapping up," she began. "My clinical rotation supervisor connected me with the Medical Director of hospice care, who wound up hiring me and, in the process of working together for about three years, became my mentor. He was always generous with his time and would listen to my ideas and take them into consideration. But the thing I appreciated the most about him was that, more than just being a mentor to me, he was a sponsor and an advocate for me at work. Instead of just supporting me and building my confidence by encouraging me, he made it clear that he knew I could do good work and gave me opportunities to apply the value he said that I brought to the team by leading meetings and driving some of the decision making.

"I think I earned my seat at the table, but as you know, just because someone earns something doesn't mean they're given those things or the opportunity to take things to the next level. My mentor did that, though. He made sure to give me a seat at the table that I deserved. He let me run meetings at work. He also taught classes at the University of Pennsylvania and would some-times bring me with him because the topic for that class session was aligned with my role at work. Instead of simply bringing me along and having me sit in the back of the classroom for the major-ity of class and speak for just a couple of minutes, he actually let me lead the class session and teach it. He was always committed to doing the right thing, even when he didn't have to, and I think giving me opportunities like leading meetings and teaching classes are examples of that. On top of everything else, I really think that helped drive the mentorship relationship forward, to a point now where I genuinely consider him a true friend."

In interviewing Alicia's mentor, he told me, "Conversations between mentors and mentees are great, but far more important is being able to give the mentee an opportunity to shine in actually doing the work. This can be scary, because failure is a possibility. I was never really worried about failure with Alicia because she's just so bright, energetic, thoughtful, and a wonderful problem solver. But in general, mentors need to be okay with a mentee potentially failing, and they have to be patient and understand that failure is a part of growth and development. The mentor has to make sure their mentee is able to cope with failure and learn the skills to pivot and adjust. This can be hard for people and preclude them from giving mentees opportunities to demonstrate their skills, but I think that's counterproductive. Instead, mentors should be thoughtful about the types of opportunities they can give to mentees where there's a high chance they'll succeed. That'll help them build their own self-confidence while also making sure you're playing an important role as a mentor by offering them opportunities to shine."

Chad Smith also sees the link between offering opportunities to your mentee and building their self-confidence. "I've talked a lot about authentic confidence, and at the end of the day, an absolutely necessary step for mentees to gain and build authentic confidence is through trial by fire," Chad told me. "Your mentee has to see if the skills they developed that their mentor facilitated wind up succeeding in the moment. Whether it's a life test, a professional experience in business, an athletic competition, or something different, you gain authentic confidence when you get to try something and succeed at it. Sometimes the outcome won't go as you want it to, and in these times, you still realize that your confidence increases because you *know* that you were prepared and that you recognized the situation ahead of time; it was just that the outcome didn't work out, which sometimes happen. That's really where authentic confidence is built."

Another mentor supported this line of thinking, stating, "I think it's important for me to not just give people a list of things to do, but to give them options and opportunities to enact their own plans so they take some level of ownership over their personal growth and development. If they're given those opportunities along the way, when they come out on the other side after having realized their growth potential, they'll get a personal reward out of it. They'll think to themselves, *I did this!* rather than, *I did what this other person told me to do.* It gives mentees a sense of self-worth and self-confidence because they have evidence that they can succeed. Then they can use that evidence of personal success as a springboard to being self-sufficient in their problem-solving skills and capacity to build a better future for themselves. After all, what any great mentor wants is for their mentee to be able to succeed on their own!"

CHAPTER 9

QUALITIES OF GOOD MENTORS

So far in Part III, I have outlined the behaviors of good mentors: exercising patient persistence, offering perspective, and developing the problem-solving process of your mentees. Just as in Part II for mentees, I want to provide mentors who are reading this with an outline of the qualities of an ideal mentor. These qualities were identified by the mentors and mentees I interviewed, which means that this chapter is informed by mentors who you'll want to emulate in some ways and by the types of mentees that you hope to serve with more intention, strategy, and purpose.

I want to reiterate that it takes years of dedication and practice to hone these qualities. In fact, the growth opportunities of the five qualities outlined in this chapter are never-ending—you can constantly refine and improve upon each of these abilities! As I've said, being intentional in your role as a mentor isn't easy. Practicing mentorship correctly is more than a full-time job and is in addition to the other roles you hold in your life and people you have a responsibility toward.

Even when you're not interacting with your mentee, you have to plan for the next meeting and keep them (and their needs) on your radar. You must behave in a consistent manner to build the trust and confidence of your mentee. You need to strike the correct balance between providing support for your mentee and giving them the space and autonomy to learn lessons for themselves. During this process, you will most certainly witness your mentee experience failure. There is a good chance that your mentee will not fully appreciate all that you are doing for them until years after you have provided them with mentorship (if at all), and they might not express gratitude and appreciation for your help as frequently as you deserve.

Despite all of these considerations, being intentional with your mentorship practice is well worth it because of the fulfilling relationship you develop with your mentee as you take these steps to provide them with value. Commit to practicing the behaviors outlined in the previous chapters and embodying the qualities presented in this chapter as you bring yourself to your role of being a mentor. You won't be disappointed in the results you see over time, the relationship you build with someone else, and the positive influence you're able to have on someone who benefits from your presence, voice, and guidance.

RELEVANT SUBJECT MATTER EXPERTISE AND EXPERIENCE

Nearly every mentee I spoke to said that their first filter in selecting the right mentor is to look for someone who has the relevant subject matter expertise or experience to help them with the areas of opportunity they want to focus on improving. In professional mentorship situations, this entails finding a mentor with the following qualities:

- Institutional knowledge for professional success at the workplace
- Years of industry experience to provide insights about the general landscape of the sector (as well as trends in the direction it is heading)
- Technical know-how and expertise to be able to provide project-specific feedback and recommendations
- Strong network of positive relationships with others in the

organization, as well as the industry at large, that can be leveraged to achieve success at work

The criteria for experience and expertise are somewhat nebulous and abstract for personal-life mentorship, but similar principles hold true. For example, if I'm looking for guidance on how to improve my parenting skills, I'll most likely seek mentorship from someone who is a parent. It would be even more helpful to find someone who has a child older than mine because that means they've gone through the process that I am currently facing, and I can learn from their experiences to approach my situation with more intention and strategy. Additionally, I will be able to have a higher level of trust and confidence in what they are recommending, as their feedback is based on lived experience.

As important as it is for mentees to have mentors who possess the relevant subject matter expertise and experience to help them on their path to a better future, it is equally important for mentors to understand how their expertise can help their mentee. In my interviews, I asked mentors to name the qualities of an ideal mentee for whom they would invest themselves fully. As one mentor told me, "One big thing for me in terms of what I look for in a mentee is a high level of alignment between a potential mentee's interests and my areas of expertise and knowledge. Because of how long I've been doing my job and the title I have at the organization I work for, people reach out to me, effectively looking for me to provide mentorship. I try to be as open minded as possible and meet with everyone I can. Relationship building is important in my line of work, and given how much my mentors have impacted my life, I'd love to give back to whomever I can.

"But a lot of times in the introductory meetings I have with people, it quickly becomes apparent that we just aren't the right fit for each other. That isn't anything bad, and it's not an indictment on them or anything like that. It's simply that the things they're interested in pursuing or the direction they want to go in aren't aligned with my background or what I might be able to help with. I think that, sometimes, people who are interested in practicing mentorship have such giving hearts that their passion for wanting to be a resource for a mentee gets in the way of honestly stating that they might not be the right person to provide mentorship.

"I think it's important for mentors to be as open, honest, and transparent about this as quickly as possible. If you have the subject matter expertise or requisite experience necessary to help someone, be willing to do it! But if you don't, be honest about it so you don't waste that person's time. Also, if you take that person on as a mentee, you're taking time away from others that you could really provide value for, so you're actually doing those other people a disservice by trying to provide mentorship to someone you aren't the right mentor for."

A number of other mentors I interviewed agreed with this assessment. Some took it a step further by saying that they still try to provide value by connecting the mentee with someone else in their network who might be able to help them, given their interests and background. Even if you are able to serve as a mentor for someone, there may be specific parts of your relationship or certain aspects of the mentee's interests that you might have to refer them to someone else for. In these cases, the referral of your mentee to another person in your network whom you trust and have a good relationship with provides a great deal of value for your mentee. After all, arguably the hardest thing for your mentee to do is to get their foot in the door. By vouching for them with an introduction and connection to someone else, you are instead walking with them to the door and supporting them as they go through it.

EMOTIONAL INTELLIGENCE

While nearly every mentee I interviewed said that relevant subject matter expertise and experience is the *first* filter in identifying a strong mentor, they all said that the single *most important* quality of a good mentor is the ability to demonstrate emotional intelligence throughout the relationship. Relevant subject matter expertise and experience are necessary to be a good mentor and set the foundation for a fulfilling mentorship relationship, but that by itself does not mean you will be successful as a mentor.

It's simply the first box to check before moving to the second, far more important step of evaluating whether or not you have the social and emotional skills to provide value and guidance. Anyone can gain the technical expertise or experience simply by sticking around in an organization or being in a role for a long enough time. As a result, a number of aspects of your mentorship will develop organically. The capacity building for emotional intelligence, however, requires your focus, commitment, time, and energy. Plenty of people spend decades delivering on their responsibilities as a spouse, parent, or friend without developing an ounce of emotional and social skills. This is because they never focused on intentionally evolving their capacity to embody these qualities.

The first consideration for mentorship discussed in Chapter 1 was being a "get to" type of person. Practicing emotional and social intelligence will help you be seen by potential mentees as a "get to" type of mentor. Daniel Goleman, the psychologist who helped popularize the concept of emotional intelligence, identified the following five key elements of people who demonstrate this quality: self-awareness, self-regulation, motivation, empathy, and social skills. As you increase your capacity for emotional intelligence, focus on building each of those five areas.

- Increasing your **self-awareness** will require a combination of improving your emotional awareness and self-confidence levels.

- **Self-regulation** involves practicing self-control, taking responsibility for your performance, and being open to new ideas.

- In order to **motivate** yourself (both to be a great mentor and attend to your responsibilities outside of practicing mentorship), you need commitment, initiative, and optimism.

- Exceling at **empathy** requires you to value diversity, be in service of others, and discern the feelings behind the needs and wants of the people you are serving.

- Having good **interpersonal (social) skills** includes practicing leadership, managing change, understanding and resolving disagreements, working with others in a collaborative manner, and placing a high value on nurturing relationships.

This is a brief primer and jumping-off point as you think about the work required and the path to take in order to exemplify emotional intelligence qualities. Extensive research has been conducted on the topic of emotional intelligence, and I recommend you look into the research studies and books that have been published to learn more concrete ways to add this tool to your toolbox. For the purposes of this book and its relationship to mentorship, however, simply understanding that emotional intelligence is the single most important filter mentees use when identifying a potential mentor is a great place to start. I hope this establishes the framework you use to intentionally approach the development of your mentorship practices.

GREAT COMMUNICATORS

Strong communication skills are a large part of expressing emotional intelligence, and I thought it would be appropriate to delve into this quality of good mentors in its own section. You may think that great communicators place a large premium on speaking clearly and succinctly. While this is certainly important, there are two steps in the communication process to focus on before delivering your messages to your mentee: asking better questions and being an excellent listener. The answers you receive from your mentee in response to your more intentional questions, which you then process through more thoughtful listening techniques, set the foundation for you to craft your feedback in a way that will land with your mentee.

Edgar Schein, a former professor at the MIT Sloan School of Management, has conducted research about how we can ask better questions. Through his research, Schein has outlined three types of questions we commonly ask others: diagnostic inquiry, confrontational inquiry, and process-oriented inquiry. More importantly, Schein has advocated for a fourth approach to asking questions that he labeled *humble inquiry*, which he described as, "the fine art of drawing someone out, of asking questions to which you do not already know the answer, or building a relationship based on curiosity and interest in the other person." Simply put, humble inquiry results from being dependent on someone else to accomplish a task you are jointly committed to. I have stressed that mentorship is a joint process that is co-created by mentors and mentees. As you ask questions of your mentee, be more intentional about what you ask, when you ask it, where you ask it, and your underlying attitude as you ask your questions. Don't focus on practicing humble inquiry at all times, as you will be most effective in your role as a mentor if you can employ the four types of inquiry where each is appropriate.

I asked mentors I interviewed about their approach to the initial conversations with their mentees. A number of them discussed questions they ask in order to get to know the mentees better and help inform how to go about building the relationship. The following are a few questions you might consider asking potential mentees when you first meet with them and gauge what the next steps are:

- What brings you joy?
- What do you enjoy about what you are currently doing?
- What are you most excited to learn about or do in the future?
- What do you truly desire?

A lot of mentees have never reflected on their answers to these types of questions, while others are in the process of discovering and refining their thoughts about these questions. Simply asking these types of questions, particularly early in the relationship-building process, can add a tremendous amount of value to the mentee's life. However, asking questions is only one part of the process. Plenty of people can ask interesting, thought-provoking questions. Unfortunately, a lot of times nothing actionable results because the person asking the question isn't committed enough to listening.

As explained in Chapter 1, consistency is the second-most important behavior for mentors to practice (after being a "get to" type of person). The third-most talked about trait from the interviews I conducted was the need for a mentor to be a spectacular listener. This not only involves listening without judgment but also having the ability to listen to the "music beneath the words" and finding the deeper meaning behind what the mentee is saying. While it is important to let your mentee have their own voice and explain things from their perspective, one of your roles as a mentor is to help them identify the root of what they are talking about (rather than what might be a surface-level indication of what they are feeling or thinking). A useful framework to consider as you think about developing your listening skills are the four levels of listening identified by Otto Scharmer, a senior lecturer at the MIT Sloan School of Management:

1. Listening by *downloading*: reconfirming old opinions and judgments

2. *Factual* listening: listening with an **open mind**, noticing what is different and noting disconfirming data

3. *Empathic* listening: listening with an **open heart**, leading to seeing the situation through another person's eyes and establishing deeper emotional connection

4. *Generative* listening: connecting with our **open will**, leading to connecting with an emerging future of possibilities

If you are intentional about your usage of the four types of inquiry highlighted by Schein and your consideration of the four levels of listening identified by Scharmer, you are setting yourself up for a successful relationship with your potential mentee. While a lot of people focus on how to deliver their recommendations in a clear and succinct manner, you will benefit by starting from a place of looking to improve the types of questions you ask and how you listen *before* you start crafting your feedback. Doing so will actually help to inform your messaging and communication approach and make that process easier.

HUMILITY

My first step in conducting the interviews for this book was to reach out to people who felt that they had a good mentor in their life. After interviewing these mentees, I asked them to connect me to their mentor so I could gain insights from a mentor's perspective. I would have an introductory call with each mentor to explain the nature of the project and tell them that I am reaching out because the mentee I interviewed had identified them as their mentor. A pattern that jumped out to me during this process was the level of humility (and honestly, utter disbelief) that each of the mentors had when I told them that, of all the people their mentee could have connected me with, they named them as the mentor that I should talk to. I repeatedly heard responses such as, "Wow, that really means a lot to me! I don't even think of myself as their mentor!" and, "To be honest, they've taught me more than I've taught them . . . They're such a great person and would have been successful no matter what. They didn't need me at all."

In a lot of cases, mentorship relationships develop organically. The two people involved don't use the labels of mentor and mentee, and often there is a delay of over a year before each person starts to realize (at least internally) that part of the relationship involves some level of mentorship. However, you're reading this book to learn more about how to be intentional with your mentorship. There is nothing wrong with wanting to be more strategic in how you act, and there is certainly no issue with having a goal of wanting to be a better mentor. You just need to be sure that you are intentional about the level of humility you bring to your role. Keep in mind that, just because you are serving as a mentor to someone, it doesn't necessarily mean that you are perfect. Be open to the idea that you don't have all the answers. Consider that while some solutions or approaches might work for you (or have worked for other people you have mentored in the past), they might not be the right answers or methods for the person you are currently mentoring.

Just as mentees are expected to have a growth and learning mindset, the same applies when serving as a mentor. You should remain open to the idea that you might get considerations from your mentee that cause you to refine your own thoughts on certain topics or situations. You should also be humble enough to learn new things. In fact, you are likely to encourage your mentee to be excited about learning something new. If you are to "walk the talk" (Chapter 8), you need to model this behavior for your mentee so they see alignment between the recommendations you give and how you are living your own life. Lastly, consider that, when it's all said and done, your mentee might achieve more success than you. In fact, more than just being open to this possibility, make this one of your goals. This not only creates a path for a reciprocal relationship in which you benefit from the perspective and feedback from your mentee, but will also potentially lead you to witness the impact your mentee has as they pay your mentorship forward to others.

PLAN AND PIVOT

The final quality of a good mentor is the ability to strike the right balance between planning and preparing for a fulfilling mentorship relationship and pivoting from your best-laid plans to pursue an approach that is more beneficial to your mentee. You must be prepared for your role as a mentor, particularly if you are providing professional mentorship. This preparation includes doing the necessary research (either about your mentee, the topic they want to discuss, or reflecting on things they may have said the last time you spoke or observed them in action). You also might need to have an idea of others in your network who might be better aligned for a specific point of your mentee's development. All of these considerations come back to the idea that was echoed by nearly ever mentor I interviewed: the mentorship process needs to be focused on the mentee. This means that you are doing whatever is best for your mentee rather than just doing what you know how to do or are comfortable doing.

Part of being mentee-focused is a willingness to pivot quickly from the plans you have laid out if they are not right for your mentee. This is particularly difficult for many people to do if they have spent a lot of time, energy, and resources preparing for these plans. It's hard for people to not view all the effort in preparing as a "waste" when they have to start on a new path. Again, you need to make sure you remain mentee-focused and do what is best for them. Sometimes, this might entail abandoning the path you're taking. Instead of viewing the preparation for that path as wasted, feel secure in the fact that your goal is what's best for your mentee, *not* what is easiest, most efficient, and most effective for you as a mentor.

As you are building the relationship with your mentee, pay particular attention to how they learn. This will help you be intentional about how you can best help them. Pivoting away from your plans will likely happen more often early in the relationship. A lot of the ideas and feedback you have for your mentee will be based on assumptions you make because you don't have all the information you need. As you witness your mentee taking actions, and you have more conversations and engagement with them, you'll get a clearer picture of how to approach the relationship and what truly is best for your mentee. As your relationship grows, so too will the effectiveness of your recommendations, strategies, and plans, thereby limiting the number of times you'll need to scrap your approach and pivot to something new. Don't forget that mentorship is a process that is built over a long period of time. Stay committed to the hard work, both in terms of the preparation required to build intentional plans as well as being willing to shift gears and pivot to something new when needed.

I hope Part III has been insightful for you as you think through your strengths and areas of opportunity related to your ability to serve as a strong mentor. With the information already presented, you can triangulate the findings from the perspective of both a mentee (Part II) as well as a mentor (Part III), in addition to considerations for the overall process (Part I), to inform your intentional approach to mentorship. You may be thinking there are some areas related to mentorship that I haven't touched upon yet. The next chapter goes into some of these areas in more depth.

PART IV

OTHER SPECIAL
CONSIDERATIONS

CHAPTER 10

FILLING IN THE GAPS

As I said in the Introduction, the enormity of mentorship makes it impossible for any single research study or book to cover every aspect. However, I don't want to leave you with an incomplete picture by omitting concepts and pieces of mentorship from the discussion. You must consider all parts of the mentorship process to be as intentional as possible in your approach to developing deep relationships with a potential mentee or mentor. This chapter will fill in the gaps by providing a brief overview of the six main limitations of my research. I am providing these not only for you to keep on your radar as you move toward practicing intentional mentorship but also as a jumping-off point for anyone interested in investigating mentorship further and conducting their own research to add to the field.

CULTURAL CONTEXT

While I am extremely proud of the diversity and representation in this research study (interview participants, the types of mentorship investigated, and topics discussed in each mentorship relationship), this research was conducted only with participants from the United States. Therefore, the insights, themes, and recommendations made throughout this book are limited in terms of their application. Keep this in mind if you are interacting with a mentor or a mentee who holds cultural values and norms that are different than those of the United States.

If you are mentoring someone who has different cultural values, remember that mentorship should be *mentee-focused* and adjust to what makes them most comfortable. The findings from this book provide a useful framework for your approach, but don't hesitate to pivot away from any recommendations that don't seem to be landing with a mentee, particularly if you sense that it's due to cultural differences and preferences on how to approach mentorship. If you are receiving mentorship from someone with different cultural values than those of the United States, practice the humility and openness required of good mentees and don't take their approach personally if it doesn't align with what you are used to. In fact, because one of the biggest pieces of value that mentors can provide is the perspective that they offer, you can learn a lot from a mentor who is from a different culture than you. Developing your cross-cultural capacities and cultural intelligence is one of the biggest areas of opportunity for your growth.

It would be interesting to discover which findings from this book hold across cultures and which ones differ. Do all cultures value consistency by both mentors and mentees? Do mentees who are from a different culture still place a high level of value on being able to observe their mentor in action? In which cultures would it be counterproductive for mentors to be open, vulnerable, and honest about challenges and failures they have experienced? If you have a more international network or specific cultural knowledge, you might be the right person to add value to the field of mentorship research by conducting your own international study and debriefing the findings.

FORMAL AUTHORITY DYNAMICS AT WORK

In my research, I interviewed participants who had no formal relationship at work (essentially, the mentees were precluded from identifying their direct supervisor as their mentor). I wanted to focus on investigating why some relationships between mentors and mentees work, even when they don't *have* to. Part of the responsibilities of a boss is to provide some level of mentorship to their direct reports. But does the boss only practice mentorship because it is part of their job description? Is the direct report only listening because their mentor is their boss, and they feel obligated to do so? Does the relationship work because the boss is a good mentor, or because the mentee is just trying not to rock the boat and collect a bonus check? In order to get around these complications (and many more), I stripped away any power dynamics that could be at play and only interviewed mentor-mentee pairs that grew about organically and informally.

Some of you reading this book may be doing so to learn how to be more intentional and effective as a mentor at work because that is part of your responsibilities as a supervisor. If this is the case for you, there are some considerations you should keep on your radar in addition to the findings presented in the previous chapters. For example, I stated that mentors should help their mentees feel comfortable with failure, and that is a much easier goal to accomplish for a mentor who does not directly supervise (and thus complete performance reviews for) their mentee at work. Because of this added layer to your relationship with a direct report, there is more difficulty in the mentee admitting things that they don't know or areas in which they need help; after all, another one of your responsibilities as a supervisor is to assess your direct reports' fit on your team and performance in their role. You can work as hard as possible to create a comfortable environment, psychological safe space, and culture of accepting the failures and challenges associated with growth and development, but those actions still might not be enough for your mentee to overcome the fear of revealing to their boss what they don't know.

While you should still work to create as safe of an environment as possible for all your team members, you can also create indirect means for your employees to receive mentorship. Focus on developing the mentorship skills of those who are in higher job titles or have been on your team for a longer tenure. Suggest colleagues on other teams for your employees to connect with, particularly those who have skill sets or institutional knowledge that can be helpful to the growth and development of your direct reports. Research on the details of what effective mentorship looks like in *formalized* relationships is an area of opportunity to add something new to the field of mentorship. I encourage you to think critically about how you might approach the research design and operationalize the variables in a study that addresses this specific portion of mentorship if you are interested in delving into it more deeply.

I received an email from a participant after our interview in which he provided a few more thoughts on the topic of mentorship. His insights directly address another consideration to keep in mind if you are practicing mentorship in a formalized role with someone at work. "I think mentors need to avoid the appearance of favoritism when choosing who to mentor. Essentially, mentors need to make sure that they are perceived as mentoring a person, not creating a protégé," he said. "In addition to the toxic effects of perceived favoritism on the junior workforce, in many cases, a senior 'mentoring' one or more individuals is as much a form of creating a power base or a loyal cadre as it is an effort to develop the potential of individuals. That can lead other senior peers to view mentoring as a threat.

"At my organization, they established a relatively short-lived and not very successful 'mentoring' program, wherein several seniors would officially offer to mentor up to three juniors. This had some inherent disadvantages in that some of the would-be mentors were supremely unqualified, and some were doing it only because management had made it a favorable evaluation bullet. The same applied to the recipients of the mentorship. The mentoring tended, in my opinion, to be artificial and contrived."

As with anything, even a program with the best of intentions can quickly devolve into a counterproductive exercise with the wrong incentives. As this mentor's email noted, a number of incentives are present in a formalized mentorship process that you must avoid. Do not engage in a mentorship program as a means to add a bullet to your performance review (this applies to both mentors and mentees). If you are a mentor, make sure you approach the role *intentionally*. You can do real damage if you are unqualified for the responsibility required of you in this position. It's also important to not build blind loyalists as mentees who advocate for you and your causes, or simply repeat your opinions and thoughts throughout the organization. That is not true mentorship and is certainly not mentee-focused in its approach, as you are benefitting much more from people who consider themselves an extension of you rather than their own person benefitting from your guidance and perspective.

GROUP MENTORSHIP

Another aspect of a formalized workplace mentorship process that was not explored in this book are dynamics associated with group mentorship. Because of the informal and voluntary nature of mentorship engaged in by the interview participants in the research study, the findings and recommendations in this book are for mentorship relationships that occur in a one-on-one context. As a supervisor at work, however, you might be responsible for multiple direct reports. While you might set up time for one-on-one meetings with each individual to support their growth and development and practice behaviors associated with individualized consideration, group dynamics will be present and will inform your approach to mentoring each of your direct reports.

If you give too much time, effort, or attention to one specific person or small handful of people, it can lead to resentment and the unintentional creation of an "in" group and an "out" group within your team. As a mentor in scenarios where group dynamics are present, you need to be keenly aware of not only how your approach is being received by the individual you are interacting with but also how your methods are being interpreted by others who have a level of insight and the opportunity to observe your style. Your employees and team members will always default to trying to find what your actions mean for themselves, whether or not your actions are actually directed toward them specifically. It's not hard to see that, as the person with a position of formal authority who determines merit increases/bonuses at work, you might be biased toward more positive outcomes for the mentees you are giving more attention to. Keep this on your radar, and stay committed to explaining the "why" behind your actions to all your team members when appropriate. Take special care to ensure that you don't default to a "squeaky wheel gets the grease" policy in which the most difficult or challenging team members receive the highest level of your attention. One main area of focus should be to develop a strong level of trust with each individual you supervise/mentor, as well as to have a strong overall level of trust within your team.

At the same time, mentees in group mentorship contexts must understand the distinction between equality (everyone receiving the same time/resources/attention) and equity (everyone receiving what they need for their own growth and development). Early in your relationship with your supervisor, give them the benefit of the doubt in terms of their leadership style, and give them a moderate level of your trust. Don't expect them to be able to explain the "why" behind the reason they might be spending more time with other employees or team members (it would often be inappropriate for a supervisor to divulge why they believe a person might require more attention).

Throughout the relationship, focus on figuring out whether you feel as if you can trust your supervisor by taking advantage of opportunities to observe them in action and take note of ways in which they have demonstrated they are trustworthy. If, over time, you believe that your supervisor has consistently shown (through both words and actions) that they can be trusted, practice self-regulation and self-monitoring in times when you are not provided explanations behind why your supervisor is seemingly spending less effort or time with you or is being harder on your than on others. Default to the thought process that they still have your best interest at heart and will be committed to fair and equitable outcomes to the entire team, yourself included. Try to practice these behaviors as much as you can, but if you still feel pulled to engage in a conversation about this topic with your supervisor, do so in a humble and open-minded manner.

Mentors and mentees alike should be committed to contributing to a strong culture of equity and inclusion within their team.

Just as mentorship is a two-way process, the creation of a team/ organizational culture is a product of the efforts of each individual. If the team you work on places a high level of value on every person being committed to equity and inclusion, it will be easier to understand the varying levels of time being given by the supervisor as "meeting people where they are and giving each person what they need," rather than an opportunity for unfair outcomes to arise. Each party in a team environment has a responsibility to create a foundational level of trust between the supervisor and each team member, as well as to collectively be committed to the ultimate goals of the team.

Research projects require a clear understanding of the level of analysis being investigated. For the study that led to this book, I looked only at the individual level of analysis. Opportunities exist to explore mentorship at the group and/or organizational levels. I think this section of the chapter provides a jumping-off point for aspects of group mentorship to consider and to try to measure. These considerations might also help to inform your research design and approach. I think a great deal of valuable data, insights, and recommendations can be added to the field of mentorship with a study that focuses on these high levels of analysis.

FAMILY MENTORSHIP

Formal authority and group dynamics also can play a role in personal-life mentorship when it comes to the process of mentorship between family members. For this reason, I did not interview any mentor-mentee pairs who were immediate family members. At the end of each interview, I asked the interviewees if they had anything else to add to our discussion. One person I interviewed, who had been identified by their mentee as a personal-life mentor, said, "I think looking into mentorship within families would be interesting. It was humbling to hear that I'm viewed as a mentor for someone else in their personal life. I met her when she was in college, and to think that she feels like I've had a positive influence on her means a lot to me. But while she's able to be open to thinking that I can add value to her life, my own kids are pretty resistant to that. It's really hard to mentor your own kids sometimes, and it's a little bit upsetting when someone who isn't a family member is saying I bring value to them, but my kids don't view me or what I'm saying as having that same type of value.

"I'm sure part of it is that I'm just Mom, and that I have a role in that," she continued. "Sometimes, it's really hard not to look at my kids and see them as the babies or the toddlers or the young children that I have images of in my mind. After all, I was with them since literally day one. So, I'm sure my approach could be better, and I'm sure I'm impatient with them at times and don't communicate with them as well as I do to non-family members who seem to value my input and my thoughts. But I also wish it weren't as hard to provide mentorship to my own family. After all, others are identifying that what I say is helpful and useful in their lives. I wish my kids would feel that same way more often!"

This discussion hit me pretty hard because, as I value my family a lot, it caused me to reflect on all the times when I wasn't open to listening to the mentorship and guidance that my parents offered (I probably *still* don't listen to them as much as I should). I encourage you to reflect on opportunities you might have had to receive mentorship from family members (not necessarily only your parents, or even family members who are older than you), and think about how you might have benefitted if you had been more open to considering their feedback. If this is the case for you, I encourage you to commit to staying more open to the possibility that your family might be able to provide you with insights and recommendations that others might not be able to. I would also encourage you to keep the recommendations for mentees made in the previous section about group mentorship in mind if you have siblings, cousins, or others who are receiving mentorship from family members as well.

If you are trying to provide mentorship to a family member, remember that a high level of patience is required of any mentor. In my post-interview discussion with the mentor who talked about family mentorship, we talked about how organic relationships require a high frequency of informal meetings to maintain the momentum of relationship building, but the opposite is true for family mentoring. Families often see each other too much or know too much about each other, and they would benefit from having more space between them in order to get the message to land. One way of doing this is to accept that, as a family member, it might be difficult for your voice to be the one that lands and makes an impact.

Again, mentorship must be mentee-focused. If this is the case and this is the goal you are ultimately committed to, then you should be intentional in seeking out a potential mentor for your family member whose voice *will* land with them and be considered. This is an indirect way you can provide mentorship for someone you are close to without fighting an uphill (and possibly unwinnable) battle to have your feedback be considered. You might not be the right person to motivate your family member to take school more seriously or consider a particular career path, but you might know someone whom they will listen to that you also feel confident can present these messages in a way that you trust. I would also recommend that you don't give up entirely on building a relationship with your family member so you can be there for them in a mentor capacity when they are ready to receive your feedback. Don't forget that there is often a long delay between people receiving mentorship and when they're able to fully understand the value of all that their mentor has done for them.

Family mentoring faces similar complexities and challenges for research that formal authority dynamics at work (as well as group dynamics) present. However, if you're able to figure out a way to operationalize a research study around this specific topic, I think there would be a high level of interest in the findings, particularly by those who would like to provide mentorship to their family. Think critically about how you would go about investigating the group level of analysis and all the nuances of family relationships to measure as you design a potential research study for this topic.

IDENTITY REPRESENTATION

Many of the interviewees stated the importance of a shared belief system and set of core values for there to be a meaningful relationship between a mentor and mentee. There is understandably a relationship between the belief system, values, and outlook you have and the identities you hold, as these identities impact the experiences you have and the lens through which you view the world. As a result, there were noticeable patterns in mentees and mentors valuing representation (sharing important identities) as part of the mentorship process. Shared identities between a mentor and mentee are useful in creating space and navigating certain details of a lived experience that don't need to be explained. This is important not only for visible diversity indicators (cultural identity) but also for non-visible ones (such as if you grew up in a single-parent household, lost a parent early in your life, etc.).

As one of the interviewees explained, "I think more important than sharing an identity is having an *emotional attachment* to that identity, and then feeling understood by someone who has a similar emotional attachment to that same identity. Sometimes, feeling understood without having to explain all the details about yourself is the nicest feeling in the world. Emotional attachment goes deeper than merely sharing identities; it creates meaning and makes you feel like you belong. It not only makes you feel heard and understood but it makes you feel like someone is connecting with you on a deeper level."

Representation of identities helps to inform your approach to finding a mentor with relevant subject matter expertise and experience. While aspects of this expertise might be purely technical (such has having the technical know-how on a project or having the industry experience necessary for providing useful insights into career opportunities), part of the value is also the experience of how a shared identity intersects with your goals.

I found that a lot of mentees valued finding mentors who shared important identities in sectors where the mentee is part of an underrepresented group (for example, Black students in highly ranked MBA programs or women in a STEM field). However, there were two interviewees who added some nuance to this. "I definitely think my mentor and me sharing important identities was of value, but I also think I'm really intentional about keeping diversity in my life," said one mentee. "As much value as a shared identity brings, I'm very much aware of making sure that my network of mentors isn't *only* filled with people who share the same identity. I need to be thoughtful about what it means to keep a diverse set of voices in my life, particularly in terms of diversity of thought and diversity of problem-solving approaches."

"No one person can be your everything in mentorship," a mentor told me. "Having only one mentor in your life isn't mentorship; that's discipleship. I don't think people should engage in that. I'd rather have mentees look at it as having a team of mentors, or a team of consultants, each of whom provide unique value in their area of expertise and add their own unique perspective. If that's how a mentee approaches mentorship, then it's really important for them to think about the places in which the voices in their lives are skewed: where is there overrepresentation of some types of voices and where is there underrepresentation of other types of identities? After landing on a thoughtful [and hopefully accurate] answer, they need to be intentional in filling in the gaps and finding the identities and voices that need more representation in their lives. It's a bit more complex than simply finding the same shared identities in different spaces."

I've set the stage for the importance of identity representation in mentorship (which could conceivably be labeled as "affinity mentorship"), but there is obviously much more opportunity for depth in this space. As topics such as diversity, equity, inclusion, and justice are receiving more public attention, and people are collectively making decisions as to how to approach these areas with more intention, the time is ripe for research focused on how these topics relate to practicing more intentional mentorship. Individuals and organizations alike can benefit from guidance around how to not only approach this with the best purpose at the outset but also how to act in a meaningful way.

MENTORS MENTORING MENTORS

The last special consideration is geared toward groups of individual mentors or for organizations that have formalized mentorship programs. If you are not already doing so or the process is not in place, think about incorporating a system into your practice where mentors meet with each other to discuss and debrief their experiences to help each other improve. Coaches go to clinics to learn from other coaches about new tactics, practice drills, and approaches to running a sports program. Doctors attend medical conferences to sit in on presentations by other doctors about cutting-edge medical technologies, procedures, and ways to deliver better patient care. Industry and job-specific conferences exist for individuals to contribute to the knowledge space as well as to learn from each other. Why wouldn't mentors and organizations that have formal mentorship programs do the same to develop mentorship capacities, capabilities, and practices?

While this book is one resource for practicing intentional mentorship, it's only one avenue to explore in an endless process of growth and development. Instead of just focusing on mentor-mentee interactions, think about how you can organize, structure, and operationalize a process in which mentors provide mentorship for each other by sharing their experiences.

Opportunities to gauge the effectiveness of this suggestion by using either A/B testing or a pre/post assessment exist at organizations that don't have a defined step in their program in which mentors meet as a means to develop their mentorship skills. Plans for evaluation and research should be included in the discussion when thinking about how to add this to an existing mentorship program. More important than research and evaluation, however, is an intentional and thoughtful approach to what a "Mentors Mentoring Mentors" component to a formalized mentorship program would look like. How often would these meetings need to take place? How would these meetings be facilitated? What are the group norms and expectations as you introduce this aspect of mentorship program, and how will they be communicated? What concrete goals do you have for this part of the program, and what is the timeframe for mentors to achieve these goals?

Just as the typical mentor-mentee relationship requires intention by both parties, so too should any approach to incorporate a "Mentors Mentoring Mentors" model into your practice. You will need to think through a number of details to ensure that your methods and actions are set up for success as you move toward developing your (and others') capacities for providing mentorship.

INTENTIONAL MENTORSHIP MOVING FORWARD

In the summer after my senior year of high school, I remember being so excited to start college. I was going to leave home for the first time and live on my own. More importantly, though, my main responsibility over the next four years was going to be to learn as much as I could about topics that interested me. Instead of the limited curriculum offered in high school, I was finally going to have the opportunity to follow my passions. I would be able to choose the major and minor that resonated best with me, and there would be no shortage of interesting electives to take. My primary job would be to absorb as much information as I could and come out of college four years later much smarter, more prepared, and better equipped to engage with the world.

Fast forward to the week before my college graduation. I remember sitting in my room reflecting on my undergraduate experience. I thought about all the knowledge I had accumulated over the past four years and was trying to identify the most important thing I learned during that time. Ultimately, the biggest lesson I learned during college was how little I actually know. The more I learned from the classroom over those four years, the more I realized how much there was still left to learn. What's more, I had to come to terms with the fact that, while my capacity to take in new information stays relatively constant and my breadth of knowledge increases incrementally, the universe of knowledge expands exponentially with each passing day. By definition, this means that, as a percentage of what I know about the world, I know less about life today than I did yesterday, and I will know less tomorrow than I do today.

My takeaway from this realization was, *I cannot do this myself; I need others to have a fulfilling life and leave a positive impact on the world*. This means that I need to be open to learning from, receiving guidance from, and relying on the help of others. It also means that I need to be willing to help others to the best of my ability when I can. In order to meet these demands, I need to approach the rest of my life with the goal of being an intentional mentee, as well as an intentional mentor. The research I conducted and the findings outlined in this book provide a framework for what that intentionality looks like in practice.

It's no secret that we collectively face adaptive challenges for which there are no tried and true solutions. Overcoming both our personal and societal challenges will require something greater than the efforts of individuals. In times when you can benefit from the guidance, perspective, and recommendations of others, I hope this book helps you think about how to intentionally engage with a potential mentor. For those of you who believe you have value to provide through your perspective and lived experiences, I hope you are not only willing to help others but also feel that this book helped you in being intentional with *how* you offer your expertise and guidance. We cannot do this alone. We will need each other to move toward a better future. Practicing intentional mentorship to build more fulfilling relationships is the first step in this process.

ACKNOWLEDGEMENTS

For a book about the topic of mentorship, I'd be remiss if I didn't express gratitude to the people in my circle who have also chosen to be in my corner. To my parents, thank you for all the love every time we talked about how the book was progressing. To my business partner, Dr. Elissa Haddad, thank you for the support and patience you provided as I pursued this passion project over the past year. To my friends, your commitment to our friendship helped keep me sane throughout the process of writing this book and I appreciate each of you—I hope I make that clear as often as I should.

I had the good fortune of connecting with a number of talented people who helped me get this book off the ground. Dan Horwitz and Jon Finkel could not have been more generous with their time to provide me with their insights and advice as I moved forward in the publishing process. I truly hope that I have the opportunity to partner again in the future with my extremely talented editor, Jared Evans, who improved my initial manuscript by leaps and bounds. I feel fortunate to have connected with Hannah Gaskamp, whose cover design and interior formatting brought this all together in the final stages.

Last, but certainly not least, none of this would have been possible without the amazing individuals whom I interviewed for this book. I cannot thank each of you enough for the hours of time you gave me in service of my vision for this project. I hope you feel that this book did some level of justice to the interviews you granted me. Your stories and ways of thinking have positively influenced me and informed my approach to building fulfilling relationships with others moving forward, and I hope this book has the same impact on the people who read it. A big thank you to all the interview participants of this research project (listed in alphabetical order by first name): Alicia Marini Bloom, Alvin Snow Jr., Anne Poduska, Antonio McLemore, Arvin Mosley Jr., Ashley Spivey, Ashton Pilz, Beth Shore, Bob Zellner, Dr. Bruce Loveless, Chad Smith, Chris Spivey, Dan Harrell, David Bonds, Dean Curry, Francis Williams, Harsh Mishra, Isaiah Afework, Ivonne Montano, Jarrett Austin-Thomas, Jeremy Mills, Jimmy Esposito, Dr. Joe Straton, Dr. John Gaines, Klara Firestone, Kristen Little, Marc LaPointe, Matt Bloom, Melissa Burgess, Mike Farrell, Nicole Austin-Thomas, Paige Milgrom-Hills, Pamela Smith, Rachi Wortham, Randy Novak, Rani Manoharan, Rashad Norris, Rebecca Otten, Renee Firestone, Sandy Neville, Scott Yahner, Sherry Johnson, Shyan Selah, Soo Hyun Han-Harris, Wendy Kessler, and Yattah Reed.

CPSIA information can be obtained
at www.ICGtesting.com
Printed in the USA
LVHW110747250821
696052LV00011BA/332/J

9 781087 978840